SANDINO'S DAUGHTERS

Also by Margaret Randall
Carlota
Cuban Women Now
Inside the Nicaraguan Revolution
Spirit of the People
With Our Hands
Breaking the Silences

SANDINO'S DAUGHTERS

Testimonies of Nicaraguan Women in Struggle

Margaret Randall
Lynda Yanz, Editor

New Star Books, Vancouver/Toronto, Canada

First printing November 1981
5 4 3 2 1

Canadian Cataloguing in Publication Data

 Randall, Margaret, 1938-
  Sandino's daughters

   ISBN 0-919888-34-8 (bound).—ISBN
 0-919888-33-X (pbk.)

   1. Women—Nicaragua—Biography. 2. Frente
 Sandinista de Liberacion Nacional. 3. Nicaragua—
 Biography. 4. Nicaragua—History—1937-1979—
 Biography. I. Yanz, Lynda, 1951- II. Title.
 HQ1487.R35   305.4'097285   C81-091354-2

The photograph of Luisa Amanda Espinosa (page 25) was
provided by her mother. All other photographs are by Margaret
Randall.

The publisher is grateful for assistance provided by The Canada Council.

New Star Books Ltd.
2504 York Avenue
Vancouver, B.C. V6K 1E3
Canada

Printed in Canada

*For the women and men who with their
lives defeated the old Nicaragua...
and to all those who with their lives
are creating the new one.*

Contents

Preface

This book is being published at a time when the Nicaraguan Revolution is facing a serious threat from the "destabilization" policies being promoted and financed by the Reagan administration. Since the overthrow of Somoza in July 1979, there has been constant military activity on the Nicaraguan-Honduran border, and Somoza's son has maintained an army base with the remnants of the National Guard. Recent reports indicate increases in military manoeuvres and in the numbers of U.S. and Honduran troops involved. These occurrences signal the urgent need for developing a broad international movement to oppose any foreign intervention in Nicaragua.

Sandino's Daughters is, in this sense, an important tool. In the first place it is virtually the only book-length account of the Nicaraguan struggle available in English. But more than that, it is an account of participants themselves— women who fought to defeat the Somoza regime and who now carry on the fight to rebuild a new and free Nicaragua. It is a different kind of history: women speaking for themselves about their own experiences as women, and at the same time analysing the process of political development in their country. What is perhaps most striking about the voices recorded here is that they force us to stretch the notion of what is political so as to include issues usually hidden and dismissed as personal.

The importance of *Sandino's Daughters* extends beyond the struggle in Latin America. These Nicaraguan women tell us how they have organized as women; beyond that, they reveal their commitment to integrate their own liberation movement with the more general struggle of people fighting against oppression. The relationship between women's liberation and socialism, or as it is sometimes posed, between feminism and marxism, has long been debated in the women's movement. *Sandino's Daughters* situates that debate in an actual practice. These women restate again and again that the option of women's liberation separate from the revolution was not a reality in Nicaragua. The process of the revolution itself created the conditions that made it possible for women to break with the past and mobilize to demand full equality. Of course, the process is by no means a simple one. Each new advance in the revolution and in the condition of women not only solves old problems, it creates new ones. Yet at the same time these changes open up new possibilities...

Many people have worked on this project as it has travelled among Managua, Vancouver and Toronto being transformed from manuscript to book. David Smith, David Kidd, Leslie Cotter and Andrea Knight were the ad hoc Toronto team. Daphne Morrison, Stan Persky, Lanny Beckman, Kathy Ford, Linda Gilbert, Tom Hawthorn and Rachel Epstein contributed from Vancouver. Involvement in this project—and through it in the struggles of women in Nicaragua—has been a source of strength and inspiration to me, as I'm sure it has been to all of us.

Lynda Yanz
Toronto
October 1981

Introduction

I worked with Sandino, as a messenger.
There were no bosses, no generals. We
were Nicaraguan soldiers against the
machos. We fought for a free Nicaragua
...I haven't stopped participating, not
for a minute. I haven't cut myself off.
These bonds will last to the end. I move
on, I put the years aside and continue
fighting for my beloved Nicaragua.
 I got the news at night. I wanted to
dance. July 19—the bells tolled for joy
when the kids won the war. It seemed
like a dream, a dream come true. But
not anymore—there's so much to be
done.

—MARIA LIDIA, AGE 68

On July 19, 1979 the people of Nicaragua, led by the Sandinist National Liberation Front (FSLN), won a resounding
victory when almost a half-century of struggle culminated
in the overthrow of the repressive dictatorship of Anastasio
Somoza. *Sandino's Daughters* is about the women of
Nicaragua—the peasant, working class, professional and
bourgeois women who joined with their brothers in the
struggle to defeat Somoza. They tell us openly about their
lives—in the days of Somoza, during the Revolution, and
today as they work to build a free country. They describe
the brutality of the old regime and their participation in the

movement which finally defeated the tyrant. They speak very personally about their fears and losses, but mostly of their victory as women and as militants.

Women participated in the struggle against Somoza and for liberation in numbers unprecedented in Nicaragua and in other countries. Many women fought with Augusto Sandino, the national hero whose army held off the U.S. Marines during a six-year guerrilla war in the 1930s. Some, like Maria Lidia, continued that struggle through to victory on July 19. But by far the majority of women involved in the most recent war were young women, carrying forward a tradition of Sandinist and women's militancy that was transformed and extended to allow for the full participation of women.

And participate they did, in every task imaginable. Women fought in the front lines as FSLN militants, participated in support tasks, worked undercover in government offices and were involved in every facet of the anti-Somoza opposition movement. They built a broadly based organization of women, the Association of Nicaraguan Women Confronting the Nation's Problems (AMPRONAC), which itself played a key role in organizing against the dictatorship. By the final offensive, women made up 30 per cent of the Sandinist army and held important leadership positions, commanding everything from small units to full battalions. Commander Dora Maria Tellez talked about some of the differences in the development of women's participation. "Peasant women got involved very early," she said. "They fought heroically in spite of severe repression. It was harder for women in the cities. Political women were looked down on. They were called prostitutes. But by about 1972 more and more women were getting involved. Then, later, organizations like AMPRONAC were successful in bringing together women of very different backgrounds in one organization."

As each of the women I talked with made clear time and again, it is impossible to understand the tremendous participation of women in the war of liberation without knowing something about the conditions that the majority of Nicaraguans faced. As in many other Latin American countries the most visible and brutal characteristic of life in Nicaragua was the contrast between the extreme poverty of the majority and tremendous wealth of the very few—the Somoza family was not just a symbol of the rich, but itself owned and controlled vast amounts of the country's wealth. Statistics tell something about life in Nicaragua before the FSLN victory. The unemployment rate was 22 per cent (with 35 per cent underemployment). Prior to the recent literacy campaign 60 per cent of adults were illiterate. In rural areas the figures rose to 93 per cent. University was accessible to 0.3 per cent of the population, with only 5 per cent going beyond grade five. Curable diseases were at epidemic levels. There was no medical system to speak of, with the result that Nicaragua had one of the highest mortality rates in the continent.

This poverty and economic backwardness is the underside of the development over the past 100 years of a dependent capitalist economy. Nicaragua had become a primary exporter of raw materials, particularly cotton and coffee. As in so many other "underdeveloped" countries this translates into benefits for multinational corporations (mostly U.S.) at the expense of the majority of Nicaraguans. The indigenous industry that did exist was controlled by the Somoza family. They controlled as much as 40 per cent of the total economy: 30 per cent of all arable land, the fishing, milk processing and construction industries, as well as the national airline and shipping line.

The terrible economic situation had particular effects on Nicaraguan women. For example, the large number of sole-support mothers in Nicaragua is related to the general economic situation. Faced with the realities of unemployment, poverty and insecurity, many husbands and fathers abandoned their families, leaving mothers responsible for the family's survival. In the daily battle for survival mothers would take any job. Most often their options included little more than domestic work or selling food and trinkets in the markets or along the highway. Many women were forced into prostitution.

Women have had to work, and their participation in the salaried labour force, as borne out by statistics, is extremely high. The proportion of women wage earners rose from 14 per cent in 1950 to 21.9 per cent in 1970 and 28.7 per cent in 1977. These are extraordinarily high figures for Latin America. And they reveal only a part of the picture; as is often the case in other countries, women are economically active in many areas not reflected in statistical surveys. These statistics point to an even more extreme situation.

Another indication of Nicaraguan women's participation in the economy is their average number of economically active years. In 1960 Nicaragua showed an index of 11.4 years, surpassed in Latin America only by Uruguay and Panama, both of which have higher rates of industrialization. This figure of 11.4 has continued to increase over the past decade as the economic situation in Nicaragua deteriorated. In general, figures for Latin America tend to be lower than those of capitalist and socialist industrialized nations, but Nicaragua's figures are comparable even to some industrialized countries. This comparison is all the more dramatic when we keep in mind that the average life expectancy is 53 years, 20 years less than in Canada or the U.S.

The extensive involvement of women in the revolutionary process was in part the result of their integration into the national economy. They have been continually pushed beyond the narrow domestic scene. While the Spanish Catholic tradition preached of women in the home, passive, dependent and "ornamental," the world around them demanded something else. History forced them to assume positions and make decisions which, along with their economic activity, increased their social and political involvement.

But it wasn't only economics that pushed so many women in Nicaragua to join the movement. Widespread political repression was also a factor. The brutality meted out by the National Guard, the private army set up and equipped to protect the Somozas from all opposition, was legendary even in Latin America, where repressive governments are the rule. Women of all classes responded to this repression by becoming revolutionaries.

Sandino's Daughters is about the contradictions and options Nicaraguan women faced in the process of deciding to participate in the struggle against Somoza. I talked with women from very different backgrounds—and women whose levels of involvement varied widely—about their experiences and about the involvement of women in general. I wanted to know how they began to articulate their need to join in the political struggle; how they made the decision, a decision that would affect every facet of their lives; and how they overcame the traditional obstacles thrown up by family and social prejudice.

The testimonies interweave description and analysis of women's situation in the old and now the new Nicaragua; and accounts of the struggle itself are presented alongside each woman's particular life-story—her family, schooling, social activities, religious training and so on. Some chapters focus on individual women. In Chapter Three Amada Pineda tells us about her life, and through her account we learn about the lives of thousands of other peasant women who, when faced with the brutalities of the National Guard, decided to take up arms. Daisy Zamora and Nora Astorga came from more privileged homes. In Chapters Four and Five each offers us details of the events in which she was involved and, more importantly perhaps, shares with us the hesitancies and fears she had to confront and overcome in resolving to become a full-time revolutionary.

Other chapters relate more directly to a theme or event. In Chapter One Lea Guido, Gloria Carrion and Julia Garcia each provide different pieces of the background to the building of AMPRONAC, and its development into the *Luisa Amanda Espinosa* Nicaraguan Women's Association. Chapters Two and Six take up different aspects of women's experience in the Sandinist army. Chapter Two contains the stories of three commanders, while in Chapter Six we learn of the experiences of rank-and-file women.

One theme that emerges again and again throughout the book is the relationship between mothers and children, and especially between mothers and daughters. The Sandinist Revolution was led and carried through largely by young people. Nicaraguan youth were massively involved in the struggle regardless of their sex. But among those above the age of 30 or 35, women's participation seems to far surprass that of men. Many women became involved through their children's activities. Often their first political involvement was in response to their child's arrest or imprisonment. Then support activities led to broader tasks. Sometimes the death of a son or daughter translated into an even greater involvement. There are also instances where it was the mother who politicized her children. Both these threads are taken up in the chapter on "mothers and daughters."

The participation of women in the Revolution continues today as Nicaraguans devote themselves to the tasks of "reconstruction." In the course of interviewing women about the past and their involvement in a revolution won, I also wanted to talk about the future, about the possibilities and problems of extending and institutionalizing women's equality in the new Nicaragua. Each of the women I talked with was confident about the future. All spoke frankly about the problems but at the same time assured me that there was no going back. Women showed their strength and determination in battle and were not about to retreat now.

The interviews for this book took place in Nicaragua from November 1979 through to the end of January 1980. At that point I was still living in Cuba and was invited back to Nicaragua by the Ministry of Culture. During my stay, while writing the book, I also had the support of the *Luisa Amanda Espinosa* Nicaraguan Women's Association, the Ministry of Social Welfare, and innumerable generous friends who contributed ideas, solidarity and material aid. In Nicaragua I especially wish to thank Gloria Carrion, Lea Guido, Yvonne Siu, Doris Tijerino, Ricardo Wheelock, Gladys Zalaquette, Monica Zalaquette and Daisy Zamora. Among those who gave of their time and energies in the transcription of more than one hundred tapes: Irene Barillas Montiel, Maria Elena Lopez Cerpas, Auxilio and Yves Chaix, Cesar Delgado, Arturo J. Diaz Villaneuva, Veronica Mercedes Gutierrez, Lesbia del Socorro Rodriguez Bojorje, Esperanza Roman and Tacho Sanchez. Generous help with photography came from Alfonso Zamora

("Zamorita") and his sons. I owe more, perhaps, than to any other single comrade, to Jaime Carrero Zuniga. In Cuba thanks are due to Antonio Castro, Alex Fleites, Sandra Stevenson, Maria Inez Ruz, Victor Rodriguez Nunez, Bladimir Zamora, Medea Benjamin, Ellen Rosensweig and Grandal. I have a special debt to the Sandinist National Liberation Front which—from long before their victory—permitted me the stimulus and example of its heroic people's vanguard.

Margaret Randall
Managua
September 1981

One

From AMPRONAC To The Women's Association

The Luisa Amanda Espinosa *Nicaraguan Women's Association is organizing and providing leadership in the difficult task of breaking down the barriers to women's full and equal integration into Nicaraguan society. AMPRONAC,* the current association's immediate predecessor, was organized during the last few years of struggle against the Somoza dictatorship. It successfully mobilized women both around issues of particular concern to women and in the wider struggle against the dictatorship. After the victory the association changed its name to honour the first woman member of the FSLN to die fighting—Luisa Amanda Espinosa. Let us listen while women from the association recreate its history.*

Lea Guido is Minister of Public Health in the National Reconstruction government. Her maternal grandmother sold meat, and her mother Eva continues in that trade in Managua's enormous Eastern Market. Her father also had working class roots; as a youngster he shined shoes, later became a bricklayer and still later headed construction crews. But his support for the Somoza dictatorship provided him with the chance of success, and a mere month after the Sandinist victory he left the country.

* AMPRONAC is the Asociacion de Mujeres ante la Problematic Nacional (Association of Nicaraguan Women Confronting the Nation's Problems).

1

Lea's parents were separated shortly after her birth with the result that her childhood and adolescence were spent between the two of them. This, perhaps more than anything else, explains the strange combination of experiences which resulted in her unusually rounded outlook: on the one hand, excellent private schools in Europe, and on the other, a sensitive people's wisdom acquired among the market women.

LEA: It was in April 1977 that I received a note from comrade Jaime Wheelock.* He suggested we organize a work commission to look at women's problems and work toward the creation of a broad-based women's association. The Sandinist National Liberation Front† had already failed in two previous attempts to organize women. This attempt was to be successful.

I had the European experience under my belt. I knew how a union was supposed to work, how a mass organization functioned or at least how a group like that was supposed to function. To begin with we set up a collective inside the FSLN to write something on the importance of organizing women. Remember that this was 1977, a year of tremendous repression at all levels. Really bloody repression. We knew it was important to bring women from different sectors together to deal with this problem—the total lack of human rights in the country, which was epitomized so clearly by the horrible conditions and the torture our comrades were being subjected to in the prisons.

The first meeting drew mostly bourgeois women and a few journalists. Of that initial group, only Gloria Carrion and I ended up as founding members of the association. But we valued the participation of those bourgeois women. Their class condition, and the image the dictatorship had of women in general and bourgeois women in particular, made

* Jaime Wheelock is Commandante of the Revolution, member of the FSLN National Leadership, and Minister of Agrarian Reform.

† The terms FSLN, the Front and the Organization all refer to the Sandinist National Liberation Front.

Lea Guido, Minister of Social Welfare in the new Government of National Reconstruction, Secretary General of AMPRONAC during its years of active struggle

it possible for them to go and see certain government officials. They were able to get interviews with men like Aquiles Aranda, the head of Public Relations for the National Guard, without fear of being arrested. They could also use international forums to denounce what was happening in Nicaragua.

So we held our first meeting with these women and it was very useful. But we also learned that these women had limitations. When "the season" rolled around, they'd stop what they were doing and go off to the resorts...or we'd begin to hear things like "it's taking up too much of my time..." or "it's just too hard..." We learned that we'd have to recruit more women from the petit bourgeoisie on whom we could depend.

That was more or less the way things developed while we were getting the association off the ground. In September we decided to hold a public meeting. We made our decision two days after Somoza declared a state of seige so it became something of a problem to get our executive committee together. Few women wanted to be publicly identified. At that point there was Carmen Brenes, Tere Delgadillo, Clarisa Alvarez—who later dropped out completely—and myself. We formed the executive committee and managed to bring off the public meeting.

Prior to that meeting we had tried to hold separate meetings for women working in different areas but the repression was too heavy. Some 60 women showed up for that first national meeting in October 1977. It received a good deal of publicity, perhaps because it was something new. Most who attended were bourgeois women and many of these later dropped out. But the meeting did have an impact and it was important. People gave testimonies about what was going on throughout the country—stories of repression among the peasants and of the mass murders being carried out by the dictatorship. We did follow-up by printing material denouncing the situation in the countryside.

For that first meeting we found peasant women in the North who were willing to come and speak about what was happening in the mountains. They talked about the disappearances and the atrocities the Guard was responsible for. These women were very brave. Testifying meant exposing themselves publicly. These were women, many of whom had lost two, three, four children—often their whole families, husband and all—who now bore sole responsibility for working their plot of land. Some were being forced to migrate and leave the zone altogether. We made contact with these women through women we knew in Matagalpa, women who would later organize AMPRONAC in that city.

It's important to understand that our idea for a women's association was never limited to a human rights commission. Our goal was always to get women to participate more actively in the solution to our country's social and economic problems. I remember us spending a whole night at one of our comrades' houses trying to decide on a name that would reflect this idea. We wanted a name that wouldn't limit us to human rights activities. We had already begun to see that we needed to organize an association that would mobilize and involve large numbers of women in the struggle against Somoza. In the fall of 1977 AMPRONAC became that organization: The Association of Nicaraguan Women Confronting the Nation's Problems.

Let me tell you, our policies were aggressive ones. We demonstrated against absolutely everything that was going on in the country. One of the first demonstrations after the state of seige and martial law were lifted was at a journalists' conference. We were there with our banner even though we were just a handful of people at the time. That's the way we began to make our presence felt at every event and mass meeting.

The dictatorship didn't quite know how to deal with us at first, both because certain bourgeois women were involved and because the whole thing was so new. We were everywhere. We made posters and banners—*Nicaraguans, Defend Your Rights...Know Article Such and Such...* Always with as much publicity as possible. And you know, at that point, the end of 1977, AMPRONAC only had a total membership of 25! And we were quite a mixed lot. Only two or three were members of the FSLN. I was the only one publicly identified with both organizations.

Toward the end of that year the middle-class sectors began to mobilize—the church, small businessmen, students, journalists. The balance of power was shifting. It was a busy time for AMPRONAC. We worked together with the progressive Christian movement to organize a public meeting. One thousand people turned out. AMPRONAC was at one and the same time an instigator and a beneficiary of the upsurge in mass struggle that was taking place.

We were involved in actions around Pedro Joaquin Chamorro's* murder in January 1978. I remember that first

* Pedro Joaquin Chamorro was the editor and publisher of *La Prensa*, Nicaragua's bourgeois opposition newspaper under the Somoza regime. He was a leader in the anti-Somoza activities. His assassination on January 10, 1978, precipitated massive demonstrations by the Nicaraguan people against Somoza. Although *La Prensa* played an important role in the anti-Somoza struggles for many years, it continues

day, Pedro Joaquin was in the hospital, and people began congregating. We were the only organization that had its banner ready so we placed ourselves at the head of the demonstration. There we were with megaphones, shouting our slogans. We were a small group but we took part in absolutely everything.

The whole country was mobilizing. Each sector was planning how to be most effective in the struggle. The different bourgeois groupings decided to call for a general strike at the end of January. For our part, we planned a takeover of the local UN offices by families of the political prisoners and those who had disappeared. Some of the groups involved in the strike tried to stop our action. They sent the ambassador to talk to us; they said we were going to interfere with the strike. Their idea was that nothing should break the inactivity of the strike.

The groups organizing the strike thought that it was going to oust Somoza. We knew it wouldn't. In any event, we occupied the UN offices. Our occupation lasted twelve days and on the last day we held a giant meeting of 600 women in front of the UN. Most were bourgeois women who were upset by Chamorro's death. We demanded those responsible for the murders be punished. That demand represented a victory for the association and Christian communities. The bourgeoisie only demanded justice in Chamorro's case but our demonstration went beyond that demand. Our new slogan was *Where Are Our Peasant Brothers and Sisters? Let the Assassins Respond!* Bourgeois women weren't the only ones mobilized in that demonstration. It also included women from the poorer sectors, from working class neighbourhoods, Riguero and places like that...Chiguin* came down hard on that demonstration. Our sisters fought back. When the troops

---

to be an "opposition" paper and today is a leading force in the counter-revolution.

* *Chiguin* is a central American word for child, son. *La Prensa* began calling Somoza's son "El chiguin." He headed a special, repressive force of Green Beret-type troops, called EEBI (Escuela de Entrenamiento Basico de Infanteria—Infantry Basic Training School).

bombed us with tear gas, we threw the cannisters right back at them. It was a really militant demonstration and even got international coverage.

The bourgeois-organized strike failed. At that point the people's movement didn't have the strength to carry off a general strike. The strike made itself felt but they weren't able to close down the transport or the gas stations or any other key sectors. In spite of the defeat, the strike was a turning point. From then on the bourgeoisie began losing control of the mass struggle.

I remember we got together at the home of one of our militants to analyze why the strike had failed. That was an important aspect of our organization's work. We developed a way of working together to analyze the situations and events we were involved in. We questioned the situation and our involvement in it. Why had the strike failed? What was missing? Our answer was: organization. We knew we had to organize ourselves better. Our job was organizing the women so we began the work of building a different type of organization—a mass organization. We created base committees, a legal commission that never really got off the ground, a human rights commission that only half-functioned, a propaganda commission that was the most successful and we also elected an executive committee.

Our time had come. People were spontaneously beginning to demand participation. I remember once when I went to Siuna, to the mines. The Christian communities had a broad-based project going and the FSLN was involved. Through my contact with the FSLN I was asked to come and talk about our association. It was a very moving experience. A hundred peasant women came down from the mountains on foot! We explained the general situation in the country and a commission of women was set up on the spot. Those women really wanted to get involved. That is one of many examples where our people were—you might say—ahead of their vanguard.

There was another instance. I remember a woman in Boaco who wrote us a letter. She had heard about the big meeting we'd had with more than a thousand women, so she wrote telling us she had 40 women who were interested in becoming involved. She asked us to come to Boaco and help them get organized. And that was happening all over the country. All we had to do was go and put the finishing touches on the organization because wherever we went there were women waiting for us. That's how the association began to grow. Soon we had over 1000 members.

Gloria Carrion is the General Co-ordinator of the Luisa Amanda Espinosa *Nicaraguan Women's Association. Like Lea, she worked in AMPRONAC from the beginning, though not as a public figure. She also ran a nursery school which served as a cover for an important propaganda system.*

Gloria was 26 at the time of our interview. Her background is bourgeois. There were three children in her family—two brothers and herself. After attending the religious schools common to most young Nicaraguan girls, she was sent to the United States for further study. She majored in education at an American university.

A number of different experiences and events influenced Gloria's political development. Life in the United States—with its enticing dreams and cold reality—had its effect on her, as did summers spent working with Christian organizations among the Nicaraguan peasantry. Another turning point was when her older brother Luis* went underground. And then there was the influence of her close friendship with an Ethiopian woman. Gloria talked about this relationship. "We were at the same U.S. college and we became close. We identified with one another on a cultural, political and human level—in total contradiction with the gringo *world surrounding us. That was one lesson I learned. In spite of coming from such different countries, speaking different languages, our different cultural habits, in spite of all the differences, our humanity found a common meeting ground." For Gloria the result of these varied experiences*

---

* Luis Carrion, Commandante of the Revolution, member of the FSLN National Leadership, and Vice-Minister of Defense.

Gloria Carrion, National Co-ordinator of the *Luisa Amanda Espinosa* Nicaraguan Women's Association

was her full-time commitment to the struggle against the Somoza dictatorship.

With the victory of the Revolution, the women's association in Nicaragua had to deal with the new situation. It was no longer a matter of organizing women to fight against the dictatorship but of integrating women into the

long-range process of reconstruction and change. The
association decided to change its name for the new task.
They chose the name Luisa Amanda Espinosa *in honour of*
the first woman to die fighting in the ranks of the FSLN.

GLORIA: In order to be able to talk about how we see
women's struggles today I think we have to go back a bit.
It's only been in the past maybe two or three years that you
could really talk about a massive incorporation of women in
the struggle against the dictatorship. And it's important to
point out that women's integration into the revolutionary
process wasn't an isolated thing. It took place within the
context of an entire people readying themselves for battle.
At the same time however, Nicaraguan women developed a
consciousness of themselves as women and of the important
role they could play in the fight against Somoza. And then
from this more conscious position, women began to
organize themselves and to take a position in the struggle
against Somoza in favour of the Revolution.

We have yet to carry out a really systematic analysis of
our situation, of the situation of women here, and of our
participation in the country's revolutionary process. We
have begun to talk about these things. We've compared
notes and are developing a fuller understanding of the
problems and issues women face. But there is much that we
know already.

Women are the pillars of their families. This is the most
fundamental and objective condition of Nicaraguan
women's lives, and perhaps of Latin American women in
general. We don't see ourselves *simply* as housewives, caring
for our children, attending to the duties of the home and
subordinating ourselves to our husbands. Women are the
centres of their families—emotionally, ideologically and
economically. This is particularly the case for working class
and peasant women.

Nicaraguan women make up a large percentage of our
agricultural workers, accounting for half of our
fieldworkers. In many instances they are the first to be
affected by unemployment, inflation and shortages. And it

Managua's Eastern Market

Managua's Eastern Market

is the women who face the task of holding the family together when the men lose their jobs and can no longer contribute to the support of the family. Often they are abandoned by their husbands. A large percentage of Nicaraguan women have been left alone with their children. Left to support their families, women are forced to take any kind of job just to be able to make ends meet. Selling fruit or bread or whatever. And somehow they manage.

Eventually we are going to have to do a statistical study of all this, but at this point our experience shows us that the majority of women share the situation I've described. And that's why we say that women in our country, and in countries like ours, are a powerful force in society—not only because women numerically make up half the population, but also because of their crucial economic role.

Women's involvement in the revolution is a result, in the first place, of their class condition. Working class and peasant women have been very involved in the revolutionary process. These women have had to fight each day for the bare necessities of life. They've had to struggle just to survive. And these are the conditions which pushed them to become involved in the Revolution. Women have become aggressive, developed tough characters. They are capable of making sacrifices.

Of course it's important to note that women's participation in the struggle crossed class lines. It wasn't only terrible economic conditions that prompted women to become involved. Many women from privileged backgrounds also took up the struggle. The widespread repression, and in particular, the way this repression centred on our youth, outraged women from all classes. The repression was so bad that it was a crime just to be young. Age alone was reason for being persecuted. We had outright political assassinations of children eight, nine, ten years old—like the case of Luis Alfonso Velasquez.* And there

* Luis Alfonso Velasquez was a Managua boy who joined the FSLN at the age of seven. He organized classmates, spoke at university rallies, collected money, made bombs and carried out armed propaganda

were others as well. Women took the lead in organizing in defence of the children and young people. Older women often became involved because of what was happening to their sons and daughters. There's a special relationship between mothers and the young. Many women began by taking part in support tasks, helping the young people and defending them against repression, imprisonment and torture. Once they were involved they would go on to other tasks.

Women's political involvement had its effect on relationships between women and men. Women began to develop their own points of view on issues and began to express their ideas. In homes where both the husband and wife lived together new relationships developed. Women started to make their feelings and opinions known. They would disagree with their husbands on issues where they never had before. And as women got involved in activities outside the home their time was less fully devoted to the home and the division of labour within the family began to change. All this demanded a re-evaluation of the family situation. And our women's movement became stronger through this whole process.

LEA: March 8, 1978 was the first time that we celebrated International Women's Day with specific demands for women. A women's organization had existed in the Socialist Party*—the International Organization of Democratic Women—but it had very little connection to the majority of women. It was a party organization, not a mass organization. They usually celebrated March 8 with a

actions. On April 29, 1979, before his tenth birthday, he was gunned down by one of Somoza's henchmen. A large park has been built in the centre of Managua and named after him. It opened to the public on the first anniversary of his death.

* This is the party in Nicaragua which is affiliated with the Communist Party in the Soviet Union. It was founded in June 1944.

program against the nuclear bomb, a program with little relevance to Nicaraguan women's situation.

In 1978 women celebrated March 8 throughout the country. Because of the extent of repression, we decided it would be best to take advantage of the slightly freer atmosphere that existed around the church. We celebrated March 8 through church masses and then after mass there was a speech. We used this method to rally women everywhere. Occasionally, we held meetings in the churches, taking almost clandestine precautions. And that March 8 was the day our comrade Nora Astorga participated in the revolutionary execution of "Dog" Vega—one of the worst torturers in the National Guard. She was a member of our association.*

By April we were working much more closely with our base committees. We took part in a hunger march in Diriamba, a march of peasants which was violently repressed by the Guard. One of our comrades was wounded; she had half her foot blown off. There were children killed as well.

Our participation with the peasants in that demonstration was very important for the association. It set off a lot of debate. The bourgeois and petit bourgeois women within the association—who were in the minority by this time—began to question our allying ourselves with the peasants. Through the debate we clarified that our association could no longer remain an amorphous and independent entity. We had to take a position on the national crisis. There were two very different political trends developing and we would have to choose between them. One was a kind of Somozaism without Somoza which in the end would result in "modernizing" the dictatorship. The other option was the Nicaraguan people overthrowing the dictatorship. We debated these two positions through continuous meetings in local committees. Then we held a large meeting with delegates representing our by then 3,000 members. We decided to join the recently formed United

* See Chapter Five for Nora's account of this event.

People's Movement.* Only about six or seven women voted against the motion; all the rest were clearly for it.

In August the dictatorship raised the prices of a whole series of consumer goods and the association began to mobilize people. We launched a campaign around the slogan *Our Children Are Hungry, Bring Down the Cost of Living*. In several cities women demonstrated in the streets with aprons and empty pots. At the same time women in other Latin American countries were beginning to organize, particularly around the problem of political prisoners who had disappeared in Chile, in El Salvador and in Argentina. This issue touches women in particular; it involves their sons, daughters and husbands.

The traditional left parties had been unsuccessful in mobilizing women. We were successful because we learned how to involve women in the national struggle while at the same time organizing around problems specific to women. We always looked at the situation from a woman's point of view. If we hadn't, what meaning would it have had for us to organize women? We might as well have been any other kind of group—a parents association, a union, whatever. If we were going to organize women our association had to be different from groups that organized other constituencies. None of the other organizations could provide women with the same kind of political space. Young people had their associations of young people, their student associations, or they belonged to the FSLN. We had many, many women who weren't going to participate in the struggle unless we could provide ways for them to organize as women.

We even politicized May 30. Mother's Day had always been a purely bourgeois day. That year we circulated leaflets pointing out how women are always commercialized and objectified. Our slogan was *The Best Gift Would Be A Free Country*. It allowed us to connect our protest as women to the struggle against political repression. One of the events

---

* Towards the end of the struggle Movimiento Pueblo Unido (United People's Movement) was formed as an umbrella organization for anti-Somoza groups, including the FSLN.

we organized was a meeting at the local stadium where women from the different neighbourhoods put on skits. "Our Children Are Hungry," for example, was about the high taxes people were being forced to pay. All the skits focused on the mothers' role—a seemingly traditional approach but capable of mobilizing huge numbers of women.

By August 1978 you could feel something brewing. The commercial sectors put forward the idea of another strike. The situation seemed better than when the last strike had been called. The United People's Movement was going full force with the FSLN participating through its student organizations. Strike preparations began. Then on August 22 the attack on the National Palace took place.* That event accelerated our plans. We knew that if we didn't keep events moving the repression would wipe us out. I don't remember if the second national strike began on the 26th, 27th or the 28th.

During the strike our association learned to function in an emergency situation. We learned how to keep going, keep operating, no matter what kind of situation we found ourselves in. We suspended the base committees with their headquarters in the neighbourhoods and organized a more centralized structure. We developed a chain whereby only one comrade from each neighbourhood would have contact with other areas. Only the leadership met together. We also modified our leadership structure; there was no longer a president, only a co-ordinator in charge of finances and others in charge of security and health. This clandestine operation was crucial to our survival through this period of increased struggle and repression and into the future.

The association began changing its organizing priorities with the first insurrection in September 1978. We felt that

* On August 22, 1978 an FSLN commando, led by Eden Pastora, Hugo Torres and Dora Maria Tellez, entered and occupied the National Palace where the legislative branch of the government was in session. Hundreds were taken hostage and later exchanged for the release of political prisoners, a million dollars and the publication of a manifesto. This was just prior to the partial insurrection of September 1978.

the situation had changed qualitatively and it was no longer a priority to organize only women. The immediate task was to mobilize everyone against Somoza. We began organizing civil defence committees, which later, after the war ended, became the Sandinist Defence Committees. We provided the neighbourhoods with wood block mimeos, organized first-aid courses and supply depots for basic foodstuffs...

Julia Garcia is 26 years old. The first time we spoke she was in her last weeks of pregnancy. The next time we saw each other the baby, her fifth, was seventeen days old. She'd only stopped working long enough to give birth and was now back at work. I interviewed Julia in Sandino City. Sandino City is the name given by its residents to what used to be known as Open 3, an extensive slum area that sprang up on the outskirts of Managua when thousands were left homeless by the 1972 earthquake. Sandino City is Julia's home and workplace; she lives in a small wooden house next door to the Sandinist Defence Committee office.

JULIA: My mom died when I was thirteen. She had sixteen children: eight boys and eight girls. After my mother died my dad married another woman and abandoned us completely. So I had to go out to work right away. I worked cleaning a factory and earned 50 *cordobas* a month. I'll tell you, I never set foot in a school because I had to work... I only began to read and write after I got involved in the struggle.

Before the victory you couldn't say publicly, "I belong to the Sandinist National Liberation Front." People were scared. But I got involved. A comrade from the Democratic Workers Committee spoke to me; he raised my consciousness about how important it was to organize and fight for a better life. I told him I wanted to learn to talk to people, to tell them how we felt and to explain how we were exploited. My first activity was occupying a church for a hunger strike. I wanted to find out, for myself, what it was like to be involved. I told myself maybe I'd learn something and get rid of my fears.

Julia Garcia and her family

One International Women's Day there was an event here in Sandino City—when it was still called Open 3—and I was invited. The meeting was on a Tuesday. That's when I began to work with AMPRONAC. I went to the first meeting and kept going and going. Two or three months later the comrades in the neighbourhood elected me co-ordinator.

I learned to read and write in the struggle itself. I knew as soon as I got involved that I was going to have to learn to read and write or else I wouldn't be able to take notes or anything. I remember one meeting when I had to bring a report written by another woman. I was really ashamed. I said to this woman, Zoila, "Look, comrade, I have this problem. I don't know how to read." But she said, "Don't worry we're not as interested in women with lots of education as we are in women with a strong commitment." That's when I started working on learning to write. I found a pencil and people to teach me. I'd take a paragraph, memorize the letters one by one, and begin to write. That's how I learned.

It wasn't easy being politically active with my kids and all. I nearly abandoned them, not because I wanted to, but in order to fight for what we have now. It wasn't just me taking part; there were lots of women. Hard as it was, we had to figure out how to participate. And believe me, it was hard. For instance, when we were organizing the civil defence committees we had to meet in little tiny rooms— sometimes there would only be space to stand—and we could see the patrol cars going by on the street. We'd have to talk real quiet, in that little room, trying to plan our role in the war...

Things moved fast: the civil defence committees, the mountains...and the victory on July 19 when we came home...triumphant! I cried from joy seeing everyone out in the streets. I remember shouting *"Patria libre!"* We were free! I was so happy to be home again; I'd soon be seeing my husband, my comrades who had been fighting in other areas, my children. My husband and I had been separated for quite a while. He'd fought in Managua and then took part in the retreat to Masaya. When we saw each other on

A peasant woman near Leon

July 21 we both cried. *We had won.* Before, when we talked about what it would be like, I'd tell him that the best thing would be if we both came out alive so we could tell each other where we'd been. And that's exactly what happened. He told me about his experiences and I told him about mine, because I was there too...

LEA: Here in Sandino City like everywhere else women were trained in war itself. For example, it was women who first noticed that the Guard was using the same men in Masaya as they had in Esteli, Chinandega and Leon. This came out through the association's assemblies. We always included detailed reporting of events or incidents our members had witnessed. It was clear that women were very observant and later we learned how to take advantage of this.

The partial insurrection in September radically changed the situation in Nicaragua. For our association this was a period of making the organizational changes necessary for

In December 1979, the *Luisa Amanda Espinosa* Nicaraguan Women's Association held its first national assembly, attended by women from all over the country.

the final onslaught. The dictatorship thought it had destroyed our movement but we had gone underground and were using the time to assess and analyze the situation so we could participate more effectively. We shored up our operational structure, held seminars, distributed a lot of propaganda and re-established national contacts that had been lost. Many people were afraid; some vacillated; others dropped out altogether. But in spite of all this we managed to hold together a dedicated core of women.

We had always understood the role we might play as a

base of support but we hadn't sufficient time to prepare for the first insurrection. The support we were able to provide was minimal; we held first-aid courses and provided the neighbourhoods with medicines and some equipment. We weren't well enough prepared. But by October we had strengthened and improved our work. I believe that our greatest contribution was helping organize the masses. By this time all our neighbourhood women knew how to organize people, which was something that many of the students, for example, didn't. AMPRONAC stood out for its mobilizing and organizing capacities.

We participated in general campaigns that the United People's Movement initiated and in specific campaigns that we women were better equipped to handle. One such campaign was the call to the Guard's families. We sent anonymous letters to guards' wives in the neighbourhoods urging them to convince their husbands that they were betraying their neighbours and the people of Nicaragua. We set up clinics—well, maybe the word "clinic" is a bit much, but we did organize houses where medical attention could be meted out during the war. We gave intensive first-aid courses in semi-underground conditions. We promoted massive innoculation programs, knowing we'd have thousands of wounded. We set up a number of neighbourhood groceries which were covers for storehouses of basic foodstuffs: rice, beans, etc.

The association became more and more radical through this period. In its language, everything. During the final defeat of the dictatorship we were part of the United People's Movement and then we joined the Patriotic Front. Nicaraguan women, through our association, had been calling for the defeat of the dictator since March 8, 1979 ...Today many of the women who came up through the ranks of AMPRONAC have important political and organizational responsibilities.

*The women's association in Nicaragua is named for Luisa
Amanda Espinosa, the first FSLN woman militant to die in
battle during the revolutionary struggle. Luisa was
murdered by the Guard on April 3, 1970. She was 21 years
old. I talked to Luisa's family and comrades to find out
more about this young militant, her life, her involvement in
the Revolution, and the events leading up to her death at the
hands of Somoza's National Guard.*

ANTONIA: My daughter's real name was Luisa Antonia.
She was born in 1948. She was the last, the youngest of all
my children. I had 21 in all but only six lived. My husband
left me; he left when I was pregnant with Luisa, so I was
on my own by the time she was born. I washed and ironed
to get us through. And she, she was so young she couldn't
help me. My brother took her to live in Granada when she
was seven. But when she was twelve she came back home
because he gave her a bad life. He is a baker and would send
her out in the streets selling bread. While she was in
Granada she went to school some and got to the third grade.

   She returned home and began helping me with the chores,
until she found herself a husband and went away with him.
She was thirteen, maybe fourteen. But she came back again
because, like my brother, he treated her badly. She was such
a sweet girl, but she had bad luck.

ROGELIO RAMIREZ: I've spoken to a number of friends
from those years and we've all come to the conclusion that
almost no one really knew Luisa Amanda. She's become a
myth in a way. I imagine that the idea of naming the
women's association after her must have come from one of
the older women; the younger ones wouldn't have known
who she was.

   Jaime Wheelock brought her to my house one night. I
think she was coming from San Luis, in Leon. It was just
after January 15, 1970 and one of the things that sticks in
my mind is how sad she was. The FSLN comrades had been
killed in Managua on January 15 and I had the impression

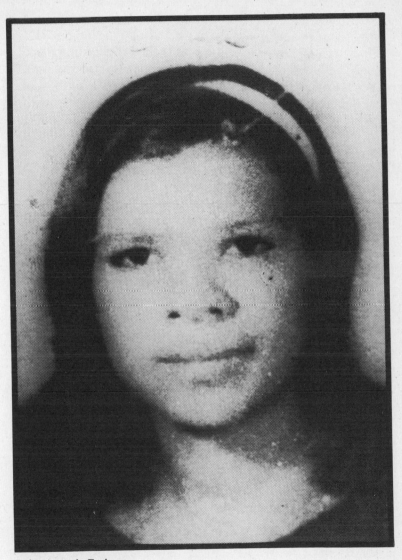

Luisa Amanda Espinosa

that she had had a relationship with one of them, Mauricio Hernandez.

I belonged to the FER* and it was an everyday affair having to hide someone in the house. A daily thing but also a very sad thing because so many of those I hid left my place to die. The fact that that kind of experience was so common makes it difficult to remember the specifics of Luisa's stay with me. But there is one thing I always remember with sadness: she was sick. I don't know what she had but I know she'd been sick for a while when she came to my house. That may have had something to do with how quiet she was. They took her from my place to the hospital.

I do remember the day she was killed. I left the house with my wife. We were walking along on the left side of the street in the direction of Merced Park. Suddenly, I saw an extremely well-dressed young woman walking along across the street. In spite of her elaborate costume I recognized Luisa Amanda. Something made me signal her, she crossed the street and walked alongside us. She spoke without looking directly at us. I asked her if she needed anything and she said, "No, nothing—I'm going to take a cab. Jot down the licence." That may have been the last security measure she ever took. She hopped into the cab and we kept walking past the park towards the Guardian Agriculture Supply House where I worked.

You can walk that stretch in five minutes, ten if you stop to talk to someone along the way. When I got to my office the receptionist said, "They just killed two guerrillas over in San Juan." I didn't know who they were, and of course I didn't know that the woman I'd just spoken with was Luisa Amanda Espinosa. I had known her as "Maura." But later I did find out Luisa was killed in San Juan. The time had telescoped so that in the few minutes it had taken me to walk to work she had driven to her death. If I had been superstitious I would have said that I saw her after her death—that's how quick it all was.

* The FER was the Revolutionary Students Front (Frente Estudiantil Revolucionario), the university-level student organization representing the line of the FSLN.

TITA VALLE: When Luisa Amanda was a member of the Organization there were very few women in the FSLN. In those days, a woman had to make tremendous sacrifices to be a member. It was the end of the sixties and the beginning of the seventies and the FSLN was going through a period of reorganization. Those were very hard years. The women who participated had to face special problems, more difficult perhaps than those faced by the men. Military tasks weren't the general rule; organizational work was what was needed. The job was to recruit people, to politicize them. Most of the women involved at that point were students. Luisa was one of the few working class women.

Luisa played the role of protecting a safehouse,* providing a secure refuge for underground comrades. It was a hard life. When I met her, her comrade—Mauricio Hernandez—had just been killed. She took it very hard; she was sad a lot of the time. And very quiet. I remember they'd bring us books to read, books that were very difficult to digest. She would read them line by line, cover to cover, in spite of the fact that she must have understood very little. She had very little education but made a tremendous effort to improve her reading and writing skills...

ROGELIO: Luisa Amanda moved out of her mother's house and went to live with a woman named Carmen. She was like her step-mother. Carmen collaborated with the FSLN. She had a small snack bar across from the San Luis Church where many of the workers from the nearby factories would come to eat. Certain members of the FSLN national leadership ate there too.

TITA VALLE: Carmen's support of the FSLN undoubtedly had a strong influence on Luisa Amanda. Living

* An anonymous place, a house with no history of use by guerrillas, where clandestine meetings can be held, the wounded can recuperate, and people can rest in relative safety.

in a house like that, where there are people in hiding, where there's a revolutionary movement going on—it must have affected her. That might have been how she first got involved. I know she used to talk a lot about her "new" mother...

When they killed her her body was at the morgue for days before anyone came to claim her. I don't know if her real mother recognized her from the picture in the papers...

ROGELIO: Carmen couldn't claim her; it would have endangered the safehouse if she had...

ANTONIA: I thought that Luisa was hanging around with the kids who got together at Carmen's house but she wouldn't tell me anything. Then one day I said—I was crying—I said, "Daughter, tell me what's the matter with you...?" She came over to me and got down on her knees and said, "Don't cry, mama. I'll tell you the truth, but you've got to promise not to turn me in..." "Turn you in where?" I asked. I told her to get up off her knees. And then she told me what she was doing. "But don't worry, mama," she said, "I can take care of myself..."

The last time she came home she hugged her sisters and told us she was going away for awhile. I gave her my blessing and she left. It must have been about a month later that the picture came out in the papers. A photograph of a man and a young woman—dead. I didn't even know it was my own daughter. I said to myself, "Good God, they killed them...how horrible." But I didn't recognize her.

The days went by. Then one day Carmen came around and left a note for me. When I got home from ironing another daughter said to me, "Mama, don't get upset about what I'm gonna tell you because we're not sure yet, but Carmen came by and left this note. She says the dead woman is Luisa."

VINCENTA ESPINOSA: One of the comrades came to the

house and asked if we were going to claim my sister's body. I told him I was afraid to, but he said I should go, that we couldn't allow them to burn her or just get rid of her. I didn't even have the money to get to Leon, but the next day he met me at the bus stop and gave me a napkin filled with more than enough money for me to get there and back.

When I got to the command post in Leon, the guards grabbed me and started interrogating me right there. They wanted to see what they could get out of me. I just said I didn't know anything. I was pregnant with one of my boys—he's nine now—maybe that's why they didn't treat me worse.

It was terrible at the morgue. I fainted as soon as I saw her and they had to take me to a hospital. Later, my niece, who had gone with me to Leon, identified the body. She knew it was Luisa from the mark on the side of her knee. And then there were those shoes; she never had any shoes of her own so my mother had given her a pair for Christmas that year. It was my sister all right.

They took us back to the command post and Colonel Adrian Gros asked me if I was going to take her back with me. "That's what I want to do," I told him, "so at least our mother can see her once more, dead." He asked if I had everything ready, the coffin and all. I didn't know what I was going to do. We couldn't afford to get her out of there.

Finally I decided to go to *La Prensa*. I went and talked to Pedro Joaquin Chamorro and he arranged everything. I didn't know him before that; I told him we were poor and didn't have the money to bury her. He said he would call The Catholic Funeral Home. At first they said they didn't do that kind of a funeral, but he said, "No matter what it costs, I want a service by The Catholic for this combatant." It cost 1,400 *cordobas* to bury someone and he took care of everything. That's how we buried my sister.

ANTONIA: They brought her home around four in the afternoon. We had permission to have her here till ten o'clock the next morning. We held a wake that night and then in the morning we took her to the cemetery. A few people accompanied us. The planes were flying overhead. We got as far as the Soluble Cafe down by the highway, when some guy pulls up in a little car. They jumped out of the car, threw a red and black flag over the coffin and drove off...

EMMET LANG: I remember once when Luisa Amanda was coming from the mountains and three guards stopped her. She was dressed as a nurse. They took her in and one of them wanted to rape her. He took her down to the river and at first she played along with him. Then, right there by the side of that river, she killed him. That's the kind of strength Nicaraguan women have...Luisa managed to get away, like she did so many other times.

TITA VALLE: I remember a time when the Guard discovered a house where comrades were hiding. They all managed to get away but the Guard kept the house surrounded. That night Luisa Amanda went back into the house through a rear window and removed a number of things they had left behind. Some arms and a sewing machine. She hid them near the river bed. A couple of days later she returned in a taxi and got everything. They weren't worth that much and she probably shouldn't have taken the risk of being caught—but she got into a cab, loaded to the gills with all that stuff and at one point was even joking with the unsuspecting guards. She got a royal bawling out for that one.

   Luisa was very committed to the Organization. She was convinced of the fact that women belonged in the FSLN as much as men did. She was a great person with a great deal of determination.

ROGELIO: There is a lot of confusion about the events leading up to her death. There were five of them in the house. Enrique Lorente was in charge of the whole zone and was also responsible for the house. The others were Luisa

"Where is Norma? Let the dictatorship answer!"

Amanda, Enrique's wife Gloria Campos, Victor Maza, and another comrade whose name I can't remember. Around five o'clock in the afternoon—on the day before Luisa's murder—they heard gunfire nearby. They naturally suspected that the house had been discovered, though later events proved that wasn't the case. Enrique got everyone together in the living room and told them they couldn't stay any longer and would have to find a way out. He ordered everyone to keep two bullets in reserve in case they ran out of ammunition—to finish themselves off if necessary. Enrique and another comrade had fallen prisoner in 1976. The very day they were arrested the Guard caught them trying to escape and tortured them. After that experience Enrique always said he'd never let them get him alive again.

The next day, when they left the house, Enrique and Luisa Amanda were together. The Guard patrol was really heavy in Leon at that time. The patrol cars were trucks with 20 or so guards. Apparently an informer saw Enrique and Luisa and suspected something. Enrique was carrying one of those airline bags with a roll of maps sticking out. The informer started following them and they must have panicked. They made the mistake of trying to make a run for it; they bolted into the patio of a house nearby and positioned themselves behind a couple of stone washstands. Aguilera, the informer, who was later executed, came into the patio and Enrique shot him in the left leg. That's when the shoot out began...

TITA VALLE: Luisa Amanda wasn't armed. There was only one pistol and it belonged to Lorente. When he fell, she picked it up and fired a volley as she tried to jump the wall. By that time there were about fifteen or 20 guards, all shooting. That's when they killed her, while she was trying to get over that wall...

ROGELIO: Some think, though it's never really been confirmed, that it was Luisa Amanda who shot Enrique. There was a woman in the patio on the other side of the wall who said she heard Enrique say, "Shoot me." Then she heard a shot. But it's never been confirmed...

EMMET: Enrique had a number of bullets in his body. He might have been shot by more than one person. But I want to point out something else: Luisa Amanda didn't go directly from the house they abandoned to the place where she was killed. Luisa Amanda was in the centre of Leon just ten minutes before she died.

ROGELIO: I know, I know, because I saw her. I told you I saw her. The only thing I can think of is that Luisa Amanda went to give a message to someone, to make a contact...

EMMET: There are two places she might have gone —Aurora's house or the safehouse that Jose Benito and Enrique were supposed to have had near where I lived. It's possible that Luisa Amanda might have gone to leave Gloria at Aurora's and then went back to get Enrique out. But we should be able to clear this up easily enough by talking to Gloria Campos. . .

GLORIA CAMPOS: I knew Luisa Amanda briefly in 1969 and then in 1970 for those last two months when we were together in that house. She was a real comrade and a joyous person; she liked to sing and dance, and yet she studied a lot. She had a tremendous desire to learn more; she read insatiably. I knew her by the name "Lidia"; they gave her that name in honour of Lidia Doce, one of the heroines of the Cuban Revolution. . .

We were expecting several comrades any minute at the house. Emmet Lang was supposed to be bringing Jose Benito Escobar and Ifrain Sanchez Sancho. We had heard gunfire so Enrique told Luisa Amanda to go to the corner and see what was happening. Luisa Amanda found a dead lieutenant and someone who could give her information about the comrades. They'd been seen in a car with an "M" licence, a doctor's plate.

Enrique ordered us out of the house—Luisa Amanda and I. He told us to go to Aurora's house. We got there around seven in the evening on April 2. Luisa was worried about the comrades at the house. So the next morning she went back to warn them that the house would probably be searched. That's when she and Enrique left and shortly after they were killed. It was my birthday—April 3. Enrique and Luisa Amanda went down fighting.

Gloria Carrion brings us back to the present. Seven years have passed, years during which many men and women have given up their lives for the Revolution. But the first

FSLN woman to die in battle hasn't been forgotten. To make sure she never will be, the Nicaraguan Women's Association bears her name.

GLORIA: Today the tasks of women and of the Revolution are one and the same. I don't believe, as some do, that women have no special demands of their own. They always had and they do now too. I think it's precisely because we've always been aware of this that AMPRONAC was able to succeed where others failed. And that's why we're changing to take on new tasks. But now women's specific demands are also the Revolution's demands. Our association is here to solve the problems women are most concerned with. Every day we learn a bit more about what women's conditions really are, what the connection between women's situation and the general condition of the entire working class—of the people in general—must be, and what intimate relationship exists between women's struggles and people's struggles.

Women making denim pants in a recently inaugurated work collective in Managua

In Leon's Subtiava neighbourhood, women are making "gofio," a traditional December sweet, which they will send to their sons and daughters who are studying in Cuba.

Our association's most general goal is to help women become involved in all areas. We want them to become totally integrated into society. This means having a presence in the political arena, in the labour force, in production, in culture and in every other area of society. We want our association to be an instrument for women, a guarantee to their fulfilling their life possibilities. Through the association women will be able to break with the obstacles that have prevented their full participation in the past.

Women here, and in many other places, are relegated to an activity not considered productive. I'm talking about domestic work. Our women assume that work individually but we believe that it is a social responsibility. It is part of the work of the society as a whole. It must be seen by everyone as work and be performed not only by women.

Men must also take responsibility for this work. And eventually, under other circumstances, people would be remunerated for this work. In any event, women must be freed from these tasks and assured the necessary time to incorporate themselves into the political process.

To be able to achieve this, men must become more aware. Not just women. The National Reconstruction government and—most especially—the Sandinist National Liberation Front are conscious of the need for women to participate actively. We have to make this possible by providing the necessary conditions. At the moment we are going over all the laws that discriminate against women.

Our association has official support from the new government. And in addition to us, the Ministry of Social Welfare has a program for women. Current plans include the opening of much-needed childcare centres. Other initiatives involve the extension of health services to mothers and children.

Our membership now includes women from all over the country, women from different situations—peasants, workers, housewives, professionals, students. But working class and peasant women still provide the bulk of our

membership. Professional or petit bourgeois women seem to need more prodding and persuasion to understand the need for their total integration. Perhaps this is because their professional and other activities provide them with a form of personal expression. The petit bourgeois woman often satisfies her need to be active in an individual way. On the other hand, women from the poorer sectors come to us spontaneously and enthusiastically because it is through their integration in the political process that they find personal realization. Peasant and working class women find fulfillment through collective action.

Women's increased participation in many areas of work and the sharing of tasks between women and men have affected personal relationships, especially among the vanguard. We are learning a lot from these changes, but it's a long struggle. The process of change within personal relationships on an everyday basis is one of the most difficult tasks. We must undo years of miseducation, the consequences of which often escape our will or desire for change.

There were many different positions on these issues even during the struggle itself. I remember a discussion we had about Mercedes Taleno's granddaughter—Lesbia's daughter—before she was born. Lesbia was arrested, imprisoned and raped by a guard. She became pregnant as a result. Her case got a good deal of publicity and produced an intense discussion among the women and men in the FSLN. There were comrades who felt that Lesbia should abort that baby, that the child should be repudiated because its father was an assassin. I remember feeling just the opposite, that the child would be a symbol of struggle and should be the pride not only of its mother but of all of us, right? She would be the concrete manifestation of our people's fighting spirit and resistance. And of our women's decision to take part in combat. To repudiate that child—then or now—would only reflect some backward notion of male lineage. As if the paternity was all that mattered.

There are many issues involved in changing relations between women and men and in developing new values. It is a complex process born in a situation of struggle like ours.

The old ways of thinking and acting are not discarded from one day to the next. Our association has the responsibility for carrying out this long, difficult and important task in the realm of men-women relationships, as well as in the general arena of social and economic relations. It is not enough to change the structures; we must continue with a process of education, of ideological struggle.

Shortly after my conversation with Lea Guido she told me she'd like to write something specifically for the book so she could share some of her feelings about being a woman and a revolutionary with women elsewhere. A few days later, she handed me the following letter:

To think of my 32 years.

Of all that I've done, and all that remains to be done.

I realize that my greatest achievement has been aspiring to revolutionary militancy. A human being's greatest self-realization comes from her revolutionary activity. The concrete construction of a new man and woman are contained in that activity, on a daily basis. Individual problems are solved through collective effort. As a revolutionary woman, I believe this is how we can struggle in the most consistent way for the society of the future, and it's in this process of struggle—together with our brothers—that we can begin to destroy the chains that oppress us.

Revolutionary practice shows women the full measure of our oppression; it shows us its economic roots, its social limitations and the ideological justifications that sustain it. This forces us to understand that our liberation as women cannot result from our efforts alone, but that in the common struggle alongside our brothers we must play an important role as spearhead: becoming conscious of our condition, analyzing it, and fighting to change it.

Our Revolution, as well as others, represents not only our people's victory, but the victory of all oppressed peoples. That's why I believe that the participation of Nicaraguan women in the Revolution and now in the reconstruction represents a triumph not only for ourselves but for our sisters around the world. It is our job to see that our participation continues and grows. The FSLN supports us. The revolutionary government has decreed laws on women's equality. We must make sure these laws become real and vital instruments through our own organization and militancy.

Sincerely,
Lea Guido

Two

The Commanders

I Dora Maria Tellez, Leticia Herrera and Maria Dora

We are in a house in Matagalpa, a coffee and livestock producing city in the North. It's one of those spread-out houses common to all small Nicaraguan towns. We've come to talk with comrades Dora Maria Tellez and Leticia Herrera. Both were guerrilla commanders in the liberation war. Dora Maria—slight, very pale, with quick movements and gestures—chain smokes as we talk. Her deep voice reveals a poetic vitality. Leticia's appearance is more Latin American—dark skin, dark eyes. The two women are "resting" these days; their recent months' work having involved them in the occupation of Leon (Nicaragua's second largest city) and then in organizing the work of the initial consolidation of the revolutionary process. Leticia was a member of the commando that occupied "Chema" Castillo's house* in December 1974. Dora Maria was "Commander Two" during the occupation of the National

---

* "Chema" Castillo was a high-level member of the Somoza government. On December 27, 1974, he was holding a Christmas party honouring the U.S. ambassador to Nicaragua. Many important Somoza people, as well as diplomats from other countries, were attending the party. An FSLN commando entered the house, stopped the party, held the most important people hostage and demanded the freedom of a number of political prisoners, a raise in the minimum wage, the publication of two FSLN documents, and a million dollars. The action was a success. For a description of the evening, from the point of view of one of the women present who later joined the FSLN, see Chapter Ten.

Palace in August 1978. Now, political rather than military tasks await both women. Dora Maria will be working in Managua, Leticia in Leon.

There are thick shadows in the room. The ceiling lamp is too high to cast much light on the wide rockers, the olive green uniforms, the black leather boots. Leticia almost fades into the rocking chair. Her face shows months of exhaustion. Dora Maria's pale skin reflects the dim rays of light; her constantly moving hands light cigarettes, open a bottle of cough syrup, emphasize, elaborate...

Dora Maria Tellez' mother's name is Maria Dora. We looked her up in Managua almost a month after the talk with her daughter. She saw us in the small house where she lives with her husband. She's learning to accustom herself to survival, to the absence of whispers, to her daughter-commander who can once again visit for breakfast. Maria Dora is a middle-aged woman whose suffering lies hidden behind the apparently orderly life of a happy marriage and a mother's concern for her children.

The interviews with Dora Maria Tellez and her mother were conducted separately. I've intertwined their voices for the sake of the story.

DORA MARIA: In this country being born into a petit bourgeois, comfortable family implies a religious education —from primary through high school. It also implies, in adolescence at least, immersion in a specific social circle. What mattered was to have friends who belonged to the country club. As your circle expands you begin to carve your own niche. You find out what's necessary for you to become what you want to be. This is the process of finding your place in society—and if you don't find it, you're lost. It's a very alienating experience.

MARIA DORA: Dora Maria was always very open, very precocious. She had her funny ways but I never imagined she would become a guerrilla. I remember once when she got involved in a teachers strike at her school. The nuns

Dora Maria

almost expelled her. She didn't want to blame anyone else so to save the others she took the blame alone. Dora Maria always had a very strong character although she was not misbehaved or stuck-up. She was obedient, sweet. Her strength showed even as a child, and now look at her...

DORA MARIA: I remember the first question I ever asked about social class. I was six or seven. In the first grade. Why, I asked, couldn't the cleaning woman in our house go to the club. I couldn't adapt to those closed social circles, nor to the prejudices people harboured in our town. We were brought up to respect all workers—no matter what they did.

My father comes from a proletarian background. Later he worked in administration in the government. My mother is from one of those aristocratic families—"blue blood." But my mom has always worked, still does. She's a dressmaker in a small tailor shop. It's made her more down-to-earth than the rest of her family...

I worked on the school councils from the time I was in junior high. In 1969-70, the year I started, the teachers strike broke out, then the milk strike and the hospital workers strike. There had never been so many mobilizations in a single year as took place in 1970. Through the school we also took part in the 6 per cent budget campaign for the UNAN.* And there were the political strikes for the liberation of the FSLN prisoners. Almost the entire FSLN leadership was taken prisoner in 1970. We staged a strike so they wouldn't be killed. That's one reason why comrades like Daniel Ortega and Polo Rivas are alive today. Security took out its first file on me that year; I was thirteen.

But it was after the earthquake in 1972 that I became much more involved...

* Universidad Nacional Autonoma de Nicaragua (Nicaragua's National Independent University in Managua).

MARIA DORA: I began to realize that my daughter was involved in politics about the time of the earthquake. Immediately after, the students took a census of all those who had been evacuated from Managua. I really thought it was just a census, but what they were most interested in was visiting those poor neighbourhoods to see and talk to people about the conditions they were forced to live in. Later, in March 1972, Dora went to the University of Leon. Leon was what you might call a hot-bed for radical students. I was afraid that because she was somewhat restless she'd get involved in all that. So I asked her not to go. But she went anyway.

DORA MARIA: In 1972 the Front intensified its political work with the people. The work was very difficult, until the earthquake. Ironically, the earthquake and the chaos that resulted from it made political work a bit easier. Doris Tijerino, Carlos Arroyo, Mary Bolt and myself worked together here in Matagalpa. There were others but those are the comrades I can think of off-hand. We were assigned to do a census of those left homeless by the disaster. The census was really a cover for our political work. Our group was sent to El Chorizo, the poorest neighbourhood in Matagalpa. We were working under the leadership of the FSLN. Doris was already a member of the FSLN and had just gotten out of jail for the second time; I hadn't yet joined.

I finished high school and entered university. I wanted to study medicine so I had to go to the university in Leon. That's when everything changed for me. I was recruited by the FSLN. I was sixteen or seventeen. At university I worked in the student movement and took part in some semi-clandestine activities, mostly support work for the people in the mountains—buying clothes, food, supplies, securing medicines, weapons, providing safehouses.

Those were our activities then, but in 1974, after the assault on Castillo's house, the repression increased and we legal members lost most of our contact with those in the mountains.

Maria Dora

MARIA DORA: I told her to be careful. She'd wanted to
study medicine since she was a child, that was her dream.
I knew if she got involved in politics she'd lose her
opportunity for a degree. She agreed, said she wouldn't
take the chance of risking her degree. But then when the
FSLN occupied "Chema" Castillo's house, I noticed she
was very happy and excited...

DORA MARIA: I went underground in 1976. That was the customary response to the tyranny in those days. The repression was very heavy. In the North and West there were hundreds and thousands of political prisoners. I did educational work in the mountains in northern Nueva Segovia. Then they sent me back down to the city, and that's where I stayed. After the National Palace operation I had to leave the country. When I returned—it was a fast decision—it was by way of Granada, Managua, Leon and Chinandega. I was here for good by the insurrection...

MARIA DORA: She left us a letter the day she went underground. The last time we saw her was January 4, 1976. It was a Sunday. Her classes were to begin again the next day. And we never saw her again. Just imagine, I had no idea. In the letter she more or less told us not to look for her. She made it pretty clear she was a member of the FSLN. She said we shouldn't search for her because we might cause her harm by asking around. It was very dangerous to be a Sandinista.

I remember she left around five o'clock in the afternoon. She'd gotten all packed in the morning. From her bureau—she had a small drawer with a lock—she took out the ring she'd received the day she graduated from high school and asked me to keep it for her. I keep everything of hers, from the first notebook she had at the age of three-and-a-half. She gave me that ring, but I never imagined...I never expected where she was going...

She once wrote a beautiful story during her vacation one year while she was still studying medicine. She'd gotten a job through a doctor friend in the maternity ward of the Velez Paiz Hospital. One day she came home very excited because she had brought her first baby into the world; she was even spattered with a little blood. She wrote a story about that experience. When she went underground she left it on her desk in her house in Leon with a note that it was "For Dad, Mom and Negro"—she calls her brother Negro—"with love." You should see how beautiful it is, the whole story of a birth. I think I have it here someplace.

A NEW LIFE by Dora Maria Tellez

Twelve o'clock noon. We are in an air-conditioned room but the heat is rising.

I'm a little hungry and sit down on a stool to talk with the doctors and nurses while I smoke a cigarette. From here I've got a bird's-eye view of the delivery room. To the left a large row of jars line the table next to the white wall, each with its respective label: there's cotton, gauze, tweezers, gloves, scissors. Everything necessary for a normal birth. Next to the table is a small cradle, tilted slightly downwards, then a baby scale, a sink and a small basin.

In front of me are three delivery tables complete with their special accessories, separated from one another by plastic pastel-print curtains. Each has a small table beside it on which the instruments are placed, and each has its own system of direct lighting.

To the right is the entrance and almost immediately next to that is a door leading to another waiting room.

I'm just finishing my cigarette when a nurse appears through the door to the other ward. At her side is a woman with peasant features. She looks very tired. She's wearing a white gown with the hospital's initials on it.

—Another one, I hear the nurse say in a not very enthusiastic tone. We all keep quiet.

—How many children have you had? asks a doctor, standing up.

—Nine.

—Will you take her? The question is for me. I guess I better say something. I've never done a delivery. I'm just a med student and an undergraduate at that. Before regretting it I say

—Yes!

The yes was the master key to my nerves. My hands begin to tremble. I take the gloves, try to put them on and (God!) one of them tears. I take another pair—carefully—and put them on right this time.

A nurse approaches to help me into the green smock and I almost contaminate the gloves by touching the smock. I begin to feel important and don't quite know why. The nurse buttons the smock and fixes it with tape.

I approach the woman who is already in position, her legs on the small bars connected to the table.

It's time for me to muster my courage. The first fight of this human being is about to begin. He or she could become a professional, a great thinker or a poet, a lone person, a fighter, an idealist or someone condemned to the poverty and brutality of this corrupt society.

The woman is moaning again. No more time for thinking.

—Push. Every time you feel a contraction, push! Bear down.

The woman moans. The child is coming now. A little more and we've got it. Push. It's almost here.

The little head appears. I try to open space for it. I'm this baby's first contact with the world of people.

I take the head in both hands, turn it slightly, pull. He emerges. I've done it! I've gotten the baby completely out! The nurse takes the child by his feet while I clean his nose and throat with a bulb syringe. The syringe drops to the floor. They pass me another. I keep working, my hands trembling. The baby is crying! My breathing, which had almost stopped, returns to normal.

I take a clamp and press the maternal end of the umbilical cord, with another I press the other end. The next step is to break the material bond which has united the child to his mother for nine months. I cut. A stronger bond remains, the bond of love, that immense love which is difficult, if not impossible, to cut.

They take the child away. I stay with the mother, clean her uterus while pressing her abdomen. She complains a little.

Okay, now I'm done.

I feel tired, nerveless.

I have co-operated with nature to deliver a new person into the world. His life begins in a delivery room. Poverty, if not outright misery, probably awaits him. In fact he has already begun to live it.

Will his body survive? And what about his hopes?

Have I completed my mission by aiding his birth?

I must say *no*. Our work will be done when we can give these young ones a new world, a different world.

I must be committed to the birth of that new world, which like every delivery will be painful and at the same time joyous.

BABY'S DATA:
Sex: male
Weight: 8 pounds 6 ounces
Alive
Completely normal
Full of hopes for that different world
Birth certified by: Dora Maria Tellez

MARIA DORA: We supported the cause, of course we did, but that doesn't mean we weren't terrified. She was just a child, our 20-year-old baby. We never really knew where she went, until two-and-a-half years later when she was involved in the attack on the Palace. We didn't even know if she was in Nicaragua. We never received a note, a message or anything.

That period was more painful than you can imagine. Without a word...Every morning I got up early and went to the door thinking maybe they had slipped a note under it...I knew she couldn't come in person; it was too dangerous. They would kill you for the least little thing. I checked under the door every day but there was never any note. I would wonder, is she eating? where does she live? where is she? what is she doing? You ask yourself all those questions. I would have been content if only she could have let me know she was all right. I'd have been satisfied with those few words, "Mom, I'm fine." But there was nothing. Those were two-and-a-half years of anguish.

About eight months before the Palace assault we were told she was up North, in the mountains. She had been seen in a *hacienda* there. The woman didn't mention Dora's name but we knew from the description it was her. By that time the newspapers had reported her death several times. Two years after she left, a girl in the FSLN was killed. I didn't recognize the photo in the paper but a few days later I received an anonymous phone call telling me to come and claim Dora Maria's body. The radio broadcast that some comrades had identified the dead woman as Dora Maria. I went to the morgue to see if it was true. It wasn't! Then the morgue called me and said there was another body there and that this time it was her for sure, but thank God...They reported her dead again after the Palace incident, and then after the Edgard Lang affair,* but no...

When the FSLN attacked the Palace the authorities said there were three women in the commando. I had the feeling that one of the three might be Dora Maria so we went to the airport when they were leaving. And sure enough, it was her! I saw her on the bus. I was on the sidewalk at the airport when the bus with the guerrillas and hostages went by. She had her face covered but, you know, her eyes are unmistakable. Shortly after that she sent me a note from Panama.

You learn to keep going, never knowing whether your child is all right or not, and you always expect the worst. Last April the newspapers reported that the commander of Léon, a guy named Evertez, had said that he was almost positive that Dora Maria was among those killed during the Edgard Lang affair. So again I went to Leon to see the bodies. But they were already buried by the time I got there. On the way from the cemetery I met a sister of one of the dead and she said she was sure Dora wasn't one of them.

The final assault began shortly after that. We didn't know Dora Maria was in Leon until they occupied the city. Radio Sandino announced that "Dora Maria Tellez, the woman from the National Palace assault, today known as Commander Patricia, took the city of Leon." After that we were even more afraid. There was still the Guard to deal with. We were her parents so it was likely they'd come after us. That's how things were...But thank God they never bothered us.

When we finally saw her it was certainly something.

---

* On April 16, 1979 in Leon, six members of the FSLN were assassinated by the National Guard. They were Edgard Lang Sacasa, Oscar Perez Cassar, Roger Deshon Arguello, Carlos Manuel Jarquin, Idania Fernandez and Araceli Perez.

There were a lot of people in the house; everyone wanted to see her. It was very impressive. I had been expecting her since two in the afternoon. She came around five o'clock, right after the installation of the Junta at the Palace. And with so many people, well I was really excited, and nervous. But I barely got a chance to talk with her. Just a few words is all. Then they left. The first few days were hard for her. Every time she came over she seemed, well not sad exactly, but withdrawn. I imagine it must have been fatigue. After so much time in Leon, so many days of war, she must have been exhausted. But not now. Now she's the same girl who went away four years ago.

DORA MARIA: I've been a member of the FSLN for five, six years. That's a long time—full of all kinds of experiences. Those of us who have been around that long have lived through the early formation period and then also

the division* in the Organization. The split and the process
of reuniting were difficult times for us. An organization
which many of us thought indestructible and indivisible fell
apart right before our eyes. Perhaps the division wasn't
necessary, but the process that gave rise to it was—the
internal discussion of our problems, our line, our strategy
and its application to our people's struggle.

Why did we divide into tendencies? A lack of maturity,
perhaps. Our organization just wasn't prepared for a
self-critical process. Few leaders, and even fewer members,
had ever had the opportunity to talk about or pay much
attention to theory. And there must always be a theoretical
process. So, step by step, it was really hard. The few books
we did have access to—*Guerrilla Warfare* by Che, some of
Fidel's speeches, *The State and Revolution* by Lenin, your
Cuban Women Now and maybe a few more—were not
enough.

Now, as far as the tendencies are concerned, we did have
one advantage. We did split, but still had one advantage
over the rest of Latin America; the three tendencies were all
more or less still Sandinist.† That was our common
heritage and it did unite us. The Sandinism of 1934, the
Sandinism of the founders of our military organization and
the Sandinism of the heroes of the Organization before the
division. It was as though we were all born of the same
mother. We had separated, but we were branches of the
same tree. Through the whole process we maintained that
the tendencies were all part of the same organization.

While this process was going on within the Organization,

---

* In 1975 the FSLN divided into two "tendencies," one calling itself
Prolonged People's War (PPW) and the other Proletariats. Soon after, a
third tendency, The Third People (later called The Insurrectionists)
emerged. This was a period of profound ideological discussion, basically
concerning strategy for struggle. The three tendencies reunited in 1977,
and today the FSLN is a united political organization.

† Augusto Cesar Sandino, Nicaragua's national hero who successfully
routed out the invading and occupying U.S. Marines in 1934, has been
fundamental to all popular struggle in the country since that time.
Sandino and Sandinism have become more than a tradition of struggle;
they are a vital part of the national identity.

the FSLN—by that I mean the Organization as a whole—was clearly emerging as the vanguard, the leader in the struggle against Somoza. Sandinism is our national identity. And it is more than that. There are a few men and women who at a given moment in history seem to contain within themselves the dignity of all the people. They are examples to all of us. And then, through the struggle, the people as a whole reclaim the strength and dignity shown by a few. That's what Sandinism is to the Nicaraguan people. It is our history, our heroes and heroines, and our people's struggle and victory.

We were talking about the division—it was a period in which we broke with much of our dogmatism and rigidity. For example, we broke with many ideas and practices that tended to alienate women from the Organization. While this process was very positive and healthy for the Organization as a whole, it's also important to understand how and why that kind of rigidity develops.

Sometimes revolutionary organizations—in order to grow—must step beyond the immediate reality and believe in something greater. There are often blows so heavy that you have no choice but to continue believing in what you are fighting for and with even more conviction. And you can believe with such a firmness that you become rigid and unbending. Then perhaps at another moment, when you have time to really analyze the situation, you can say, no, we don't have to believe in that.

All the militants trained during that period are the same—forged in the struggle, with a tremendous commitment to the Organization and to the Nicaraguan people. That faith in the people, no one really knows where it comes from. I don't think revolutions are made by totally ordinary people. We revolutionaries are visionaries to a certain extent. That analysis may not be very formal, nor very political, but it's true.

Sometimes I wonder, I ask myself why, given the brutal repression in 1973, when the people didn't yet support us, when they informed on comrades who carried out various actions, when they pointed them out on the streets, when the repression shattered us, when thousands of people fell—why did we keep on believing? And why in 1960, in 1961, in 1963 and 1967 did the militants keep believing that one day the people would rise up?

What makes a man believe in his own potential as a man? What makes a woman believe that she is capable of anything? No one taught us. That is one of the great mysteries about the Revolution. They don't teach it to you at school. You don't learn to believe in humanity on the streets. Religion doesn't teach it. It teaches us to believe in God, not in men and women. So it's difficult to awaken that belief in yourself and in others. But in spite of all that, many women and men did develop that commitment.

It becomes an obsession—the people must rise up, they must. It begins with a vision, an imaginary idea. And holding onto that vision requires a constant process of nourishment. At first the Organization had very little capacity to analyze our people's experiences. We had to understand that people are historically capable of making revolutions, that they must and will make them—that's a historical law. But I never understood it as historical law. I think many people didn't. Of course there was the Cuban Revolution which showed us it could be done. And although we felt close to the Cuban people emotionally, we were distant as far as comprehending the mechanics of their revolution. All we knew was that we were going to make the Revolution, however long it took. Ten, 20, 30, even 40 years. Most of us thought we'd never live to see the day. It's still hard to believe that we've done it.

Commander Leticia—Miriam was her last and best-known war name—is listening as we talk. Sometimes she nods agreement. The exhaustion in her face and the heavy shadows that fill the room conspire against our talking or taking photos. Slowly and hesitantly she offers some details of her life...

LETICIA: I should begin by saying that I'm not Nicaraguan; I'm Costa Rican. My father is Nicaraguan and

Leticia

my mother is Costa Rican. As a teenager, my father crossed
into Costa Rica to get weapons and transfer comrades.
That's how he met my mother. Later he was forced to leave
Nicaragua because he'd been involved in the death of the
first Somoza. They went to live in Costa Rica. That's where
I spent most of my childhood.

My own political development began while I was still a
child. My father had a strong commitment and he
transmitted it to me. I always felt a tie to Nicaragua. I
remember that some of the FSLN founders used to visit our
home and I used to participate in their meetings. You could
say I had a very special upbringing.

I didn't attend school like other kids. I didn't go to school
till high school and right away I joined the student movement. In 1968 I got a scholarship to the Soviet Union where
I made contact with FSLN comrades. I went through training and when I returned to Nicaragua I was a member of the

Organization. I entered the country semi-clandestinely to carry out political work. That was in 1970 and I've continued from then on...

I'm 30 now, the "older generation" you might say. I have two children—the older one is almost eight. I left both of them when they were about two months old. I didn't really get to know the oldest until last year; he had been staying with his father's mother. And the youngest was born just last year. I left him at two months as well but our separation was shorter.

As far as personal relations go, I think there was and is a lot of instability. The reason for this is obvious—all the work. Work has always separated couples, and sometimes the separation is permanent. Here we value work over personal life...

DORA MARIA: Personal relationships have changed. In general I think they've improved. During a revolutionary process ideas change. This is the case with women. Women participated in our Revolution, not in the kitchens but as combatants. In the political leadership. This gives us a very different experience. Of course they played other roles during the war and acquired tremendous moral authority, so that any man—even in intimate relationships—had to respect them. A man would be hard put to lift a hand to hit or mistreat a woman combatant.

The Nicaraguan people are emerging from a war and they have been tremendously affected by it. It is impossible to see so much death and go on unaffected or unchanged by it. Death was a reality every day; you came to expect it. Not just the militants, everyone. A man would get ready to go to his office in the morning and while brushing his teeth he probably wondered if he'd make it home that afternoon. Maybe the Guard would look at him funny and shoot and kill him. People said goodbye to each other and didn't know if they'd see their friends or family again.

There are some deaths that you just never accept, not even after many years. There are people who you can never really believe are dead. It is still hard to think about our leaders who are dead. You learn to shift your feelings a little. We have internal mechanisms which help us forget this kind of thing. Otherwise I don't think we could go on living.

It's through experiences like these that our values have changed. We've had to live through things most people can't even imagine. All of this has called into question values and beliefs that used to be taken for granted. How could values not change in families where sons and daughters were killed, where a mother lost what she loved most? I mean, what *couldn't* change in a home where a woman was already capable of seeing her children fight for the Revolution, accepting their death, burying them, and then often having to pretend they were still alive so the repression wouldn't fall on them all the harder? Anything, even the role of women—so deeply rooted—can change.

Now we are at a new stage in our struggle: the massive incorporation of the people in the rebuilding of Nicaragua. It is a very different situation. In combat people give their lives. They give up everything and leave everything behind. They lose sleep, get sick, go hungry, go barefoot or whatever else is called for. But things have shifted. The tasks are different. Now the task is to work twelve, eighteen or 20 hours a day. To work Saturdays and Sundays. That's very different from giving your life. I think Che was right when he said work heroes are harder to find than war heroes. Today I'm unable to participate as a teacher in the literacy crusade or in volunteer labour as a worker. I am terribly envious of people taking the literacy census; I would have loved to participate in that. But we are involved in other things. Now there are aspects of the work we can't participate in. And that's sometimes difficult to accept.

II Monica Baltodano and Zulema

Monica Baltodano, Guerrilla Commander of the Nicaraguan Revolution, is 25 years old. Her list of experiences is long. She became involved through the usual channels for women with petit bourgeois backgrounds—the student

Monica

movement, the Christian movement and finally armed struggle.

The interview was held in her office, where Monica co-ordinates the political work of Nicaragua's mass organizations. The Ricardo Morales House was, until recently, the residence of the dictator's brother, Luis Somoza. Now, for the first time, the mansion is accessible to the Nicaraguan people and functions on their behalf.

Monica, along with two other comrades, led the final offensive in the capital and the now-famous tactical retreat in which 7,000 people marched to Masaya—liberated territory—just before Somoza's defeat. She has now left military tasks for political duties. During our conversation, the Commander's three-year-old son, Pancasan, was asleep on her lap. For Monica, as for many others, these first few months of victory have included reunions with children and families.

Zulema is Monica's mother. She has eight other children. She spoke to me in her home, also in Managua, and offered her own version of the facts and revealed how—through her children and particularly through Monica—she conquered her own fears and joined the struggle.

MONICA: I was born in Leon on August 14, the day of the little *griteria*.* Both my parents came from working class families. My father's mother was a domestic worker who got involved with her boss—or, I should say, the boss got involved with her. And my mother is the daughter of a carpenter and his wife. When I was born my father was a law student. My mother had a small shop. She put my dad through law school, working long, hard days in the shop. She had four children during that period.

ZULEMA: I identified with the struggle from the time I was very young. I knew that things had to change one day. I didn't know how, but I was aware that we lived in a time of

* *Griteria* is a popular religious festival.

injustice and that we had to rebel. I used to have arguments with my husband. Sometimes Monica or our younger daughter Amparita didn't agree with their grades so I would say, "If they don't agree, they have a right to go and complain. It is their right." I was like that. During the school sit-ins, I spent many nights at the school. My husband never backed us, never gave his support. That created problems between us and eventually led to our separation.

I have nine children. Or I should say, had nine children, one died in the war. I had two sons and seven daughters. Monica was the first to get involved. By her third year of high school she was already participating in school activities for grievances, for the political prisoners, in the teachers strike, the milk strike, and others. She was only thirteen then...

MONICA: I'm the third in our family. We were nine altogether, one after another, with a year or a year-and-a-half difference between us. My dad began working with a cotton farmer and then became one himself, in Leon. At that point, for a very short period, my dad had money. Cotton is a very treacherous way to make a living. One day you're rich and the next you're out on the street. That's exactly what happened to us. My dad went bankrupt when the Black Hill erupted and destroyed the surrounding plantations (ours included).

From then on we were poor—but it was a contradictory kind of poverty. We studied in Catholic schools, the two boys in La Salle and the seven girls in La Pureza. We were poor but attended a rich kids' school. It was awful. In those places you are indoctrinated into a completely traditional, archaic class mentality. All of us hated it. That was our life until my mom separated from my dad and we came to Managua looking for a way to survive.

I had always been a humanitarian, slightly different from my classmates and others in my family. When I was a child I wanted to be a missionary and go to Africa or some place like that. I think many comrades started off like that. Even before I was involved in anything I used to put a political emphasis on the social research papers the nuns assigned, to show that the causes of poverty were in the system and not spiritual phenomena. Then in my fourth year of high school I started my political activity. I worked on the campaign to free Doris Tijerino from prison. That's the first demonstration I remember going to. I made posters and everything; I was so excited. My friends were shocked by my activities.

In 1970, the year of the teachers strike, I was invited to Managua to attend a course on group dynamics called "Faith and Joy." It was an important experience for me. Some of the people in the course were very political and challenged the rest of us. They talked about the need to change the structure, the system. They said that poverty has social roots and doesn't come about as a result of the intrinsic evil of mankind. They were more radical than most of the people I'd met up till then.

At the end of that school year the students held a big meeting. We decided not to spend the vacation fooling around and instead to study and organize. For three months we helped build the Christian movement in our area.

ZULEMA: We moved to Managua in 1972. Monica had already graduated. She continued her involvement in the Christian movement in Managua. By then Monica was active in what they called self-examination. She worked with people in the slum neighbourhoods. By that point the Christian movement was beginning to worry the authorities and was forced to start taking security precautions.

MONICA: I was a believer. I remember how, during the school sit-in, we went every day to the chapel to pray to the Virgin to make the authorities release the prisoners. The basic issue which distinguished us from the comrades we called "communist" was whether or not liberation would require armed struggle. The priests used to say that when you got to the university, radicals there turned you on to

Marxism. To avoid our being converted to Marxism the priests promoted a highly social Christianity which was supposedly not in contradiction with social activism. According to the priests, we had to carry the voice of Christianity to the campus, and offer proof of Christian testimony.

I remember a Christian meeting we organized in 1972. A member of the FSLN spoke to us about Nicaraguan history. He gave it an interpretation I was totally unfamiliar with, that is, a Marxist interpretation. That was an important turning point for me. I was still a Christian when I entered university but I had stopped believing in all the trappings. I wanted nothing to do with rosaries or masses or anything. I still believed in God, but a God removed from the Church...

My mother was very influential in my becoming a revolutionary. In high school I defended the idea of a peaceful road to liberation. My mom would argue with me. She'd say, "No, at my age I'm convinced that we'll only win through armed struggles...." I would argue against her and then my comrades—some of whom were in the Revolutionary Students Front (FER)—would say, "the woman's right." I'd get furious. But it was she who thought like that at first. Afterwards, when I began thinking seriously about armed struggle, she drew back a little. When she saw me getting in deeper and deeper, she backtracked even further. She may have held her earlier convictions but she feared what might happen to her daughter...

ZULEMA: With Monica active in the FER, my daughter Amparo participating, and the youngest starting to take part—let me tell you, what I felt most was fear. Deep inside I knew that what they were fighting for was just, yet I felt tremendous fear. Sometimes I tried to get Monica to abandon the struggle. I would say that I didn't believe in the triumph of the Revolution. It was taking so long. By then things had calmed down again. Victory was nowhere in sight. I didn't even read the pamphlets they brought to the house. I just didn't read them. I remember one girl used to

Zulema

invite me to see plays; once we saw Gorki's *Mother*. I went
and it was all very nice, but that was the extent of my
participation.

We mothers saw the experiences of other mothers. So
many dead sons and daughters. Their deaths seemed

senseless. All the Nicaraguan people felt the same way, really. Everyone called them "the crazy kids" going off to meet their death. "How will they ever be able to compete with the Guard when the Guard is armed to the teeth?" We were convinced of that. They were right in protesting but we didn't believe they could win. Each of us thought our children would just be more martyrs.

I started to get more active around the time of the earthquake in 1973. When the earthquake struck, a group of us were occupying the Managua cathedral. There were about 40 of us from Leon. We were protesting the commercialization of Christmas. After the earthquake we returned to Leon. Monica joined the rescue and to help make ends meet I opened a boarding house. Monica was, at university then so of course the boarders she brought home were activists. So many people lived in the house during that period. I began to get more and more involved myself, by helping them. . .

There were many instances of kids being stuck in jail and then their parents or teachers would have to fight to get them out. Monica got into something like that. She was at a rally in Guadalupe and they picked her up and another comrade at about nine at night. She was only kept for about half an hour, but they opened a file on her and started following her. I remember that "Chele" Auilera, a notorious guard, followed her a lot. From that time on they didn't lose sight of the two corners of our house. We were always watched.

I was afraid, but I kept helping them. And I continued developing. I remember one incident during the Cathedral sit-in. There was a boy named Ivan Gutierrez—I don't know what happened to him, I don't think he's dead. This boy came to live at the house. They had kicked him out of his own home but I didn't know why. Monica told me a friend of hers had nowhere to go and she wanted him to sleep in the house for awhile. We put him in a room with another fellow who lived in the house. The other man smoked dope and one day the Guard came to inspect the room. We didn't object to them searching for the marijuana, which in fact they found, but I didn't know

Ivan's briefcase was full of subversive literature. Once they found that, they began searching the whole house. Monica's room was plastered with political posters. One guard left with the briefcase and another waited for the boy to come home. I told one of the kids to go to the corner and make sure Ivan didn't come to the house. I didn't have that much political consciousness then but I was sure going to protect a boy from the Guard. They never caught him.

The Guard kept showing up after that, three days in a row. We took down Monica's posters and burnt them—everything. By then my husband almost never came home. He was afraid. One day he showed up and I broke out in hives—nerves—and got a fever. So I went to lie down and my husband brought the Guard right into the room and told me to tell them Ivan's name. I said to the guard, "Look, lieutenant"—I didn't know if he was a lieutenant or what—"Look, lieutenant, don't pay any attention to this man. He doesn't even know if his kids eat because he never comes around here. How does he know if I know the name of the fellow who lived here? He can't accuse me of anything. He's better off not getting involved so I don't put him on the spot."

That was a time when many kids were leaving. They were disappearing. So-and-so wouldn't come home and I'd be told he'd gone to Mexico or France. "Come on," I would say, "don't kid me." The repression was increasing. They were clamping down on everyone. I was afraid to continue having boarders and made plans to return to Managua. We moved to Linda Vista, without Monica. I no longer put my name on the door but I did want to keep working with boarders...

MONICA: I joined the FER in 1972. The earthquake was in December and in early 1973 I was recruited by the FSLN. I think I always wanted to be a revolutionary. I remember men would say things to me like: "When we get married, I'll get you your own car and you won't have to work...etc. etc." By the next day I would be saying "no way!" I couldn't even consider that kind of life.

It was a time when there was a lot of discussion and debate about the role of women in the struggle. At an early point women in the Christian movement were more conscious than many in the FER. There were always scores of women in the Christian movement and they participated on the basis of a strong conviction. Later when the FSLN began working in the Christian movement the fact that the women involved were really strong and had a high level of consciousness had an effect on the FSLN.

The problem of male chauvinism was evident among comrades in the FER and FSLN. Some men harboured distinctly sexist attitudes toward women. They believed that women were for domestic tasks alone and that we shouldn't go beyond being messengers. There were a lot of arguments. Some comrades were open to dealing with sexism while others remained closed. Some said women were no good in the mountains, that they were only good "for screwing," that they created conflicts—sexual conflicts. But there were also men with very good positions. Carlos Fonseca, for example, was a solid comrade on this issue. It's been a long struggle! We won those battles through discussions and by women comrades demonstrating their ability and their resistance.

By 1974 I was underground. I was in the countryside, between Telica and El Sauce. I was arrested in July of 1977...

ZULEMA: We mothers have a thing about our kids, you know. We get to thinking one is more intelligent, or another is happier...So I began reading the pamphlets in an effort to find out why, even though they were intelligent, they had chosen this road, the road to death. And I assure you, it helped being more politically aware. It helped later when I had to bear up under the hard blows I received. If I hadn't been clear politically I might have reacted the way many mothers did. Some are still resentful. It's their lack of political consciousness...

When Monica went underground I went six months without news—nothing. She did leave instructions for some friends to visit me to explain the situation. By that point I had made up my mind that this was the way it was going to have to be but I still doubted that they would win. The truth is that a lot of people were dying. There were so many people killed or taken prisoner and put through the military courts...

While we were living in Linda Vista, Monica wrote me that she was pregnant. That really frightened me. One day a woman came by and started asking me questions about myself. I was suspicious and afraid, but when she came back four days later, she brought Monica and her son. Monica had sent her to check out the house. They came with the baby and a small box of clothes. Monica stayed for the day and then left late in the afternoon. She left her son with me. He was crying when she left. She had nursed him for three months and now I had to bottle-feed him. That visit was only the second time I'd seen Monica since she'd gone underground.

After that I started getting letters more frequently— naturally, there was a baby in the picture now. She told me to name him Pancasan.* That scared me; people were bound to be suspicious. We told people he was my other daughter's child, but giving him that name...My husband said, "Are you kidding? That's crazy!" and I even said "I'm going to name him Bayardo." But that night I kept thinking about it and decided no, what if my daughter dies and I haven't even given her the pleasure of naming her son. I registered him as Pancasan...

I continued to get more involved. They sent me word that my daughter didn't have enough food, that she didn't even have salt, so I started sending her things every month or

---

* "Pancasan" refers to a guerrilla experience in August 1967 in which a great many of the strongest members of the FSLN were killed in ambush. In spite of the military failure, the Pancasan experience is considered a political landmark in the struggle. The fact that the Organization survived that setback indicated that Pancasan was not a guerrilla "foco" but simply an armed struggle unit of an organization well-based in the working and peasant classes. It also pointed out the necessity of armed struggle in the struggle for liberation.

two. I joined with other comrades—Santos Buitrago* and
other women—to help the prisoners. At first we were very
timid about it and hardly did a thing. Once we were
assigned to find safehouses and people who would donate
money to the struggle. At one point I had five people, each
giving 100 *cordobas* a month.

When the baby was seven months old Monica was taken
prisoner in Matagalpa. She was held there for three months
and then the jury pardoned her. There were no charges
against her. At first they scheduled her release for October
17. That turned out to be the same day as the incident at San
Carlos, in Masaya, where several militants died. I don't
know if they had planned to let her out or not but they took
advantage of the San Carlos incident to keep her in jail.
They sent her to Managua where she was held another six
months.

After Monica was arrested I didn't care if the whole
world knew I was a revolutionary. I became fully involved.
We formed the Committee of Relatives of the Political
Prisoners. I worked to defend her with all my might. If they
even lifted a finger against her I went to *La Prensa* or to the
radio and made public what was happening. I was no longer
afraid, nothing mattered.

MONICA: When I was arrested I was working in Esteli. I
was in charge of the North and travelled frequently to
Jinotega, Matagalpa...That day we were going to a
meeting in Matagalpa and I guess someone started tailing us
after we left Sebaco. A jeep and a red Cherokee caught up
with us. They started shooting and were shooting to kill. I
don't know how the three of us managed to get out alive. I
leaped out and ran away from the highway into the fields. I
walked a whole day. Finally I had to ask a peasant for

* Santos Buitrago is Julio Buitrago's mother. Julio was the FSLN leader
who was killed when the house he was in was surrounded on July 15,
1969, in Managua. After the death of her son, Santos Buitrago became
one of the leading figures of the mothers' movement.

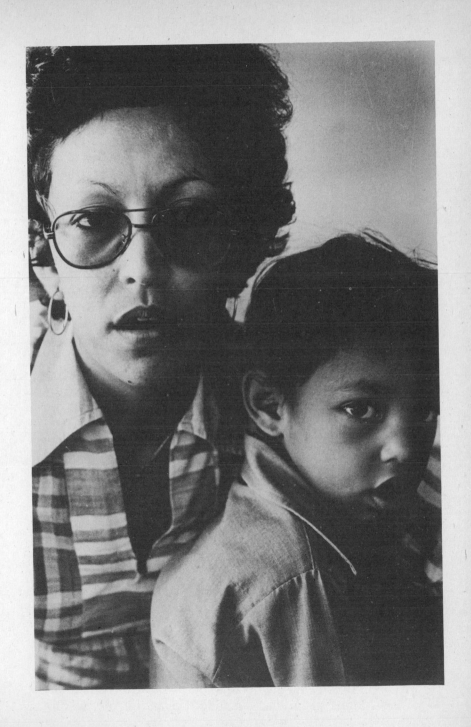

directions. He betrayed me and I was captured in Dario. I was in jail for nine months.

They didn't give me the electric shocks so many other women received. They just beat me. But the worst part of being in jail was the cell itself. The stench was so bad you couldn't sleep. They tied you to the wall and you had to sleep like that. The experience toughens you. They say it prepares you to break and finally talk, but actually it helps you grow.

There were many other comrades in the Central Jail in Managua when I arrived. They spoke to me through a little hole they'd made with a fork. They worked on it till you could see through it and use it like a telephone. I proposed we carve a big hole from the little one so we could move from cell to cell. We learned all that in there. We learned how to protest, to scream, to demand sun. They treated us even worse than the men prisoners. The men comrades had a collective kitchen, ping-pong tables, a television set...we had nothing. We were stuck in tiny cells all day; we barely managed to keep sane. We began throwing ourselves against the walls, and since the Central Jail was visited by people the authorities didn't want seeing such spectacles, we finally got them to give us sun, longer visiting hours, and other concessions. We never did get conjugal visits like the men.

ZULEMA: The entire time Monica was in jail we fought so they would give the political prisoners sun and visiting hours. I carried out letters signed by all the women; we got them out in the lids of fruit jars. Alesio Gutierrez, the head of the prison, said to me one day, "How did this letter get out of here?" I told him some guard brought it out. "Some guard we gave 20 *cordobas* to," I said. I took the letter, signed by all the prisoners, to *La Prensa*. We learned how to take advantage of that...

That's how the time went by, six months of planning, fighting and participating. We also worked with the women who were organizing the occupation of the United Nations office. That sit-in also included relatives of missing peasants. It was a great experience. Eight of us went, four from Managua and four peasant women. There was also another comrade, Cela, the co-ordinator.

The action was a protest. We women with political prisoners had no illusions that the prisoners would be released as a result of the protest. Our major objective was to mobilize and politicize the masses. The peasant women weren't as clear about what could be accomplished. There was one who broke my heart. Esmeralda was around my age, though she looked like my mother—so pained and mistreated. She would cry a lot. We didn't want her to feel deceived when the strike was lifted and our relatives were still in jail. So we started talking to her. We told her we probably wouldn't be leaving with our prisoners or missing relatives. We didn't even know where those that were missing were. In fact, we learned later that they were already dead. Four of Esmeralda's family were missing— three sons and a son-in-law. One of her daughters-in-law was there with her. She was younger and quickly understood what we were getting at. She helped us politicize the others. One day we put on some music and played "The Peasant Women of Cua" and Esmeralda said "that song is about us, that's just what it sounded like. It's true, those were the screams you could hear when they burned the houses with the people inside."

The Peasant Women of Cua*

Comrades let me tell you what happened
to the peasant women of Cua
the General dragged them from the mountains
to torture and make them talk.
Maria Venancia and Amanda Aguilar
two daughters of those hills
wouldn't rat on our rebel men.

Ay...! Ay...! we didn't see
no one for sure.

* Lyrics and music by Carlos Mejia Godoy, based on a poem by Ernesto Cardenal.

The black night swallowed
the sound of those terrible cries
Ay...! Ay...! the nation is in tears
the moans you hear
are like childbirth cries in the night...

Ay...! Ay...! we didn't see
no one for sure.
A guard told Candida Marinez
"Come here, woman,
wash these pants of mine."
The peasant girl
had to go, follow orders
while Tacho's face on a poster
mocked from the wall of the hut

Ay...! Ay...! we didn't see
no one for sure.
The *quiquisques* broke into flower
and new corn blossomed on the stalk
while the patrol took poor Mathilde
the Indian woman aborted
from interrogation
I heard all this in these hills...

That sit-in was a good experience. We were very well-organized. Chiguin's EEBI* forces made their debut by trying to bomb us with tear gas. It was after that that *La Prensa* started calling Somoza's son "Chiguin."

When the time came for Monica's release, I went to *La Prensa* again. I argued with Alesio Gutierrez, the head of the prison, and demanded to know if they were really going to release her this time. There were all kinds of problems and delays, but finally they let her go. A rally was organized for her at the university. All the students were there to hear her speak. Afterwards they said we should all go down to the Red Cross where a group of women were on a hunger strike. I was afraid all over again. How was Monica going

---

* A special repressive force under Somoza's son called EEBI, Escuela de Entrenamiento Basico de Infanteria (Infantry Basic Training School).

to go to a demonstration when she'd just been released from prison?

When the demonstration left and headed for the hunger strike we slipped away. The plan was to make sure we weren't followed. It worked. All the informers went to the demonstration. There was no one near our house. Monica went in alone, changed into a dark blouse and came out again. About two blocks away comrades were waiting for her. That's how she went underground again. So ended her prison life. I kept going to the jail. By this time I was signing in as the aunt of another woman, named Baltodano...

MONICA: After I was released from prison I worked for a while in Carazo and then later was put in charge of the Capital. I had been in charge of the North Front, so it was only a matter of learning the particular situation in Managua.

You asked me if I ever had problems in leadership because I am a woman. I think I was rather lucky in that respect. For example, here in Managua I worked with Walter Mendoza and Ramon Cabrales. I worked with comrades who have the mentalities of new men. I don't think they even thought about the fact that I was a woman. Besides, I had prestige and a lot of experience. There were some difficulties with comrades who didn't know me. Where problems did arise, it was usually with sympathizers, not members of the Organization. This was particularly the case in the North; northerners have terrible problems with male chauvinism. They saw me as a woman and not as a leader so they didn't help me as much as they helped the men.

In fact, if you were living in a safehouse in the North you knew you had to help with the sweeping, the cooking and the dishes—if you were a woman. That was my experience. I also had tons of letters to answer so I had to start at five in the morning and work until late at night. In the North we worked all day and only went onto the streets at night. Sometimes a male comrade might arrive and spend a whole day with us before heading for the mountains. He would have nothing to do all day and so could help with the dishes, but it was hard for the sympathizers to accept this. The comrade often understood but the woman of the house didn't. She would say, "How is a man going to help me?" One woman asked me, "How is it that you don't wash Bayardo's clothes if you're his wife?". . .

The final offensive here in Managua began sooner than we had planned. We even had problems transferring the weapons from the west side of the city to the east where we were going to stage the resistance. There were three of us on Managua's General Staff: Oswaldo Lacayo, Raul Venerio and me. What did I do in the insurrection here? I walked. I had to visit all the points of combat. Every day I went out walking and my feet swelled up like balloons. It was an enormous zone. I went back and forth—co-ordinating, doing political work, enforcing discipline among the people on the barricades.

After twelve days we had no more munitions. It was terrible to see the *compitas*.* Then came the decision for the retreat to Masaya. That retreat is historic, right? We had to leave with around 7,000 people, including civilians, children and militia. We divided into groups: the vanguard, the centre—where all the wounded were—followed by the rearguard.

We reached Masaya and then Carazo, where we stayed about a week. Later we went on to Granada. We went to Granada knowing that Somoza was going to resign that day. We had received the news while we were still in Masaya. We went through at dawn and fought the whole day. By nightfall we had surrounded an area known as La Polvora. I remember I even had a bath after that battle. Then the next step was negotiating with the Guard. After cleaning up we headed out. I remember a woman asking me where I was going. "To the surrender," I replied. We approached the hospital, keeping a good distance from the guardpost, moving up house by house. When we got closer

---

* *Compita* is the diminutive of *compa*, derived from *companero* or comrade. It's a term used in Nicaragua to identify a fellow revolutionary.

to their headquarters and had ourselves positioned around the building, we got word that they wanted to surrender. One of the Guard came out draped in a flag and I went to talk to him. That dialogue is taped and filmed. At first he refused to speak to me because I was a woman!

ZULEMA: Toward the end, what happened was what was bound to happen. All my children left, every last one. They all became involved in the struggle. At home we lived more poorly, but we had a solid political consciousness. Then came the time to make bombs and harass the Guard. My two youngest children were assigned to make contact bombs. That was the last year, during the Carlos Fonseca memorial.* They made bombs and painted walls. The paint for the slogans came from my house. My daughter Amparita was the most politically advanced and had a fair amount of responsibility. My son who had gone to study in Leon had also joined the Organization. Besides the two of them, another woman comrade came to stay in the house. They all did physical exercises in the house to keep in shape. And we prepared enormous quantities of food—rice and black beans, and *pinolillo*.† I made gallons of *pinol*. That's what we lived on.

In our last house I didn't pay rent for five months. It belonged to a millionaire. That's the period we worked the hardest. We lived in four different houses that year. As soon as the Guard caught wind of us and began coming by, we would move. We left no trace. Then the Guard would

---

* Carlos Fonseca, Commander-in-Chief of the Nicaraguan Revolution and a founding member of the FSLN, was killed in battle on November 8, 1976. It was a terrible blow to the FSLN and to the struggle. Tomas Borge, another of the founding members (and the only one to survive), was in prison when Carlos Fonseca was killed. When a guard came to taunt him with the news of the death, Tomas said, "You're wrong Captain, Carlos Fonseca is someone who will never die." Even before the victory in Nicaragua, November 8 was commemorated by the people.

† *Pinolillo* is a drink made from toasted cornmeal and cacao, with water. It is a standby in Nicaragua.

forget about us and we could go on working. In addition to *pinol*, there were arms, powder and bottles for molotov cocktails at the house.

My daughter Zulemita was participating in armed propaganda actions. Then she was arrested and my organizing activity began all over again. Finally on Palm Sunday they let me see her. She had two holes this big from the electric shocks they had applied. "Don't worry," she told me. She was a brave girl. Sometime later Zulemita died in a bombing, along with 200 others.

Around that time I began sleeping alone in the house. Alone with Monica's boy. I said to my other kids, "If they capture me, they're going to get me alone. I'm old." All the kids went to sleep elsewhere. They came over during the day but didn't stay the night because that was when the raids were most likely to occur. They never did raid us.

Carlos Fonseca's funeral demonstration, November 7, 1979

On Holy Thursday the comrades came by and told me that my daughter, Alma Nubia, had had an accident. Right away I knew it was serious. It must have been about five in the afternoon. They took her to a clinic and were going to call a doctor to come and operate on her but there weren't proper conditions in the clinic. She bled way into the night. Then the comrades decided to take her to a hospital. "Life comes first," they said. It was to our advantage that it was Holy Week. There weren't so many guards. They took Alma to the Occidental Hospital. At about eleven at night two comrades came back to tell me not to worry, that they had operated on her and she was all right. "Don't worry, go tomorrow and ask for Sylvia." They had registered her under her war name. I said, "Are you kidding? They'll have a guard right beside her!"

I went to see the doctor—Alma was in the intensive care recovery room—and he told me it would be impossible to visit the ward. Alma heard me arguing and began shouting, "Mom, here I am." So the doctor said, "Look, it's against the rules but that voice deserves an answer. You can see her for a minute." He was impressed by how young she was. He asked me, "How did they bring her to the hospital? They say it was a bomb..."

I went to see her and I'll never forget it. I wasn't crying but I was done in. I didn't cry so as not to upset her, right? When the doctor opened the door, she lifted her two stubs, wrapped in gauze, and said, "Look, mom, I'm alive! You see, they didn't kill me. They dropped that big bomb on me but they didn't kill me. Life is what matters. Don't worry yourself..." Already planning her cover...

MONICA: One of my sisters had her hands blown off when a contact bomb she was making exploded. The Guard was following her and I knew we wouldn't be able to get proper care for her here. We had to get her out of the country so she could be operated on. They had operated after the accident but she needed a whole series of orthopedic operations. Since there was no way to get her out legally, I told her to seek asylum in an embassy with my

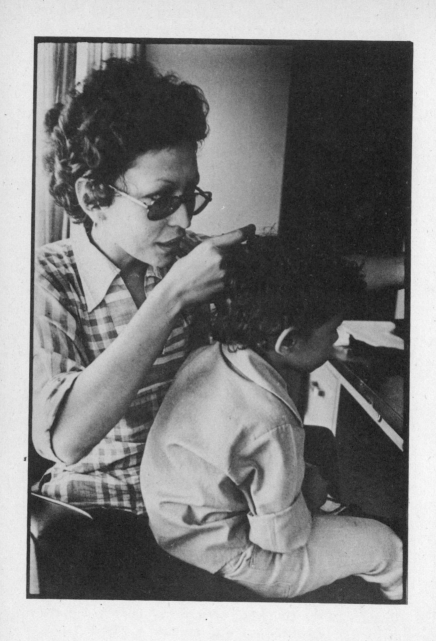

mom and baby. But the asylum took forever and I had to leave for Masaya, so I called for them to come to the liberated area. We had improvised a landing strip between Diriamba and the sea so planes could arrive with cargo. Alma left the country on one of the Costa Rican planes that had brought in munitions. They made her a prosthesis in Cuba and now she is just great. Her morale and spirit are an example to everyone. She has served as an inspiration to me in many ways.

The child begins to move and awakens. Monica tells me how she was assigned to head a battalion after the war, until she was transferred here to the Secretariat of Mass Organizations. Regarding her rank as commander, she says, "It got to the point where lots of people were being called commander. The term was becoming meaningless. Then it was decided that the rank of commander would be given only to those comrades who had acquired proven levels of experience in fighting and leadership."

Three
Amada Pineda

That night, several of them came to where they were holding me. They raped me. I struggled and they began to beat me, and that's when they did all those terrible things to me. My legs were black and blue, my thighs, my arms. I had bruises all over me. That's the way they treated all the peasant women they picked up; they raped them and tortured them and committed atrocities. It was just three days, but those three days were like three years to me—three years of being raped by those animals. They came round whenever they wanted, all the time. It's horrible—it's *nothing* like going to bed with your husband. It's not the same at all. Just before they captured me, there was a young woman who'd only been married a month. That woman couldn't even stand up when they were through with her. They grabbed one leg and then the other... I've never seen anyone bleed like that. When they let her go she had to steady herself against the walls so she wouldn't fall down. She had to hold on to the branches of the trees till she got to her house...

Amada Pineda is a woman from the Nicaraguan hills. Her gestures, her way of speaking, the simple way she dresses, the way she combs her hair, everything speaks of a woman approaching middle age who was born and bred in the countryside. She is a woman who worked with her husband in the fields and in the struggle, who had nine children, most of whom died young. Hers is the story of many Nicaraguan peasant women. But Amada's particular history includes having faced the most brutal and cruel repression of the Somoza dictatorship and having survived the ordeal. It includes travelling to the Soviet Union and Cuba; it includes airplanes, hotels, press conferences and other experiences normally outside the scope of mountain life.

This woman is not afraid to meet your eyes when she speaks. Rather, she searches them out, telling her story with calm dignity. She is seated before me, her hands folded in her lap. Only for the briefest moments is it possible to see the scars that all survivors carry with them.

AMADA: I'm a peasant woman. I was born in the hills, raised in the hills, married in the hills. We were three sisters, but there are only two of us left—one died in childbirth.

I'm 36 and have been married for eighteen years. I've had nine children; only four are left. Most of them died young, some at birth and others around the age of two. One died recently, in the war. We've always been poor and, you know, the poor fight for their children's survival. But there are times when they just can't be saved. One of my little girls died of measles, another of pneumonia up in Matagalpa. We went from one doctor to another to see if we could save them, to keep them from dying, but we couldn't. Another of my children died in the mountains when I had to flee the guards. He was just two months old. That was when they murdered the peasant leader Bernardino Diaz Ochoa and we had to go into hiding. My husband fled in one direction and I took the kids and ran in the other. My baby died in a rainstorm.

The life of the peasant woman isn't easy. She gets up at two in the morning to slap out the day's *tortillas* and to make the food she's going to leave for her children. Then she goes off to work in the fields alongside her man. She

brings him his noonday meal. Perhaps only some *pozol*—a ball of well-cooked cornmeal. That's usually all. It's not much in the way of nourishment. She's got to help her husband plant the corn and the beans. The women go out to work in the fields, with a *machete* or whatever. Often the children must be left locked in the house. The mother leaves food for them there—boiled beans with a little salt—and they just eat when they want. They're on their own. The older children help their smaller brothers and sisters. It's a life of suffering and the kids are sacrificed because that's just the way life is. Whether they have a small plot of land or work as field hands on the large *haciendas*, life is about the same.

Around 1963 we had a little coffee plot. My husband was working in the union, and though I always asked him about it he never told me anything. The comrades would come around but we didn't really know what organization they belonged to. Although the FSLN existed at that point people didn't know too much about it. Now I realize that some of the comrades who came to our house then were already members of the FSLN and were among those who later died in the fighting at Pancasan.

As I was saying, the comrades would come and help us pick coffee. They'd talk to my husband Bernardo but he never confided anything in me. I guess he thought I might give them away. I always asked about what they were doing, and I read the literature the comrades left us. Around that time I went to stay with my mother for a while. I was about to have my third child and went to stay with her so she could take care of me. With me gone, my husband devoted more time to the union.

The struggle in those days was for higher wages for the workers. They were only paying the field hands three or sometimes five *cordobas* a day. We fought for a minimum of twelve. And for plots of land for the *colonos* (that's what we call people who live on the *haciendas* all year round). And for medicines when they got sick. For outhouses. The

struggle against the landowners was gaining strength. That's when they began to call in the Guard and the repression got very heavy. The government always said there was no law against unions, but that unions brought in subversive activity.

That was when I gave birth to the child who died in the rainstorm when Bernardino Ochoa was killed. Bernardino is like a hero to us. They tortured him like you wouldn't believe: they strung him up and put a crown of electric wires on his head, they gave him electric shocks over and over, they sliced off his heels and made him walk barefoot carrying a pack. You can't imagine the things they did to him. He knew the names of all the men who were taking part in the union, but they were never able to find out who else was involved. So many men died like that.

After Bernardino was killed I began going to union meetings. Comrades from the FSLN would come to my house, I'd feed them and we'd talk. The government people always thought that by repressing us they'd fill us with fear. Instead they made us even more courageous. The repression had cracked down on us and one of my children was dead—what could I do but fight back?

My husband was a member of the Nicaraguan Socialist Party and I became a member too. I also joined the Organization of Democratic Women.* But when the repression got really bad my husband had to leave home and go into hiding. Sometimes he'd sneak home late at night, just come in and out. He'd take a look at the children and he'd be gone, back to the mountains. That's the way we lived—with the threat of the Guard always right there. The local political bosses spied on you and then the Guard appeared. Lots of peasants were taken away and we never saw them again.

When I was arrested it didn't come as a surprise. In fact, the day before, I got word—ironically, via a political boss—that they were looking for me. The political bosses

* The Organization of Democratic Women was connected with the Nicaraguan Socialist Party and affiliated with the International Democratic Women's Organization.

weren't all the same; some were worse than others. One who must have had a tiny bit of humanity in him told my father to get me out of the house. He said I should go into the mountains or to the city. The truth is, I couldn't do either. Who would have taken care of my kids? I'd have had to leave them there, and then the Guard would have taken them away. The best I could do was go to another house, a bit farther away, a bit farther into the hills. That's what I did. The house was very small and I had to sleep on the floor on a strip of plastic with one of my daughters and another woman. That night it just happened that all my kids had a fever. At about four in the morning I heard the dogs barking. They barked and barked. I got up, opened the door and looked out. The first thing I saw was a line of guards around the house, all in firing position. I closed the door and rushed to wake one of the other comrades.

I was so nervous I couldn't even stand up. I tried to get dressed but I put my dress on inside-out. But when they began to shout insults at us, that's when I got control of myself. They didn't want to break into the house; they wanted us to come out. I was tying my shoes when I heard one of the officers shout, "Okay, you bitch, when are you going to come out of there?" I called out, "I'm coming, I'm just tying my shoes; I'm not about to come out barefoot." Just at that moment one of them reached through the door and slapped me in the face. That's when I got real angry and at the same time lost my nerve.

I stayed in the house for a while, taking my time until I felt like coming out. I came out carrying my three-year-old daughter and the baby, who was just fifteen months. One of the women had given birth to a baby girl eight days before. The men in the house dragged her from her bed and made her get up. She told them she was sick and had just had a baby, but they said she had to get out. The other women were already outside by that time. That left only the men inside.

When I got outside the officer asked me my name. When I told him he said, "So you're the one we're looking for." "If I'm the one you're looking for, then you've found me," I replied. I wasn't nervous any more. "Give that kid to the old woman over there," he said. I didn't want to let my baby go. I knew if I did they'd start beating me. But at the same time I thought that if I refused they'd beat her. I knew they might kill her. The old woman was crying. "Give her to me," she said. I handed her my baby, and my other daughter too.

That's when they began to beat me. In the face, in the chest, in the stomach. They threw me against a pile of firewood in front of the house and continued pounding me. They didn't beat any of the men. It was me they were after. They asked me where I had the weapons hidden, how many weapons I had, how many guerrillas I had contact with, and if I was a guerrilla. I told them that if I was a guerrilla they never would have found me.

"But you feed the guerrillas," they said. "You take messages to Managua and bring messages back to the mountains." I said no to everything. They asked about my husband and where he was. By that time he had been in the Soviet Union for eight months, taking a course in Moscow. I told them it had been half a year since I'd seen my husband. "I'm separated from him," I said. "He ran off with another woman."

There were a lot of guards. They tied the men up. They took us away—seven men and me. I was the only woman. They locked us all together in the same room, in a house they had nearby. That was their first mistake. Kept together like that we could plan what we were going to say and tell each other what we had said in the interrogations. They started with me. The two officers asked the questions.

During the interrogation the officer told me, "Look, I don't like beating women. I was born from a woman myself. The only thing we want is for you to tell us what you know." "I don't know anything," I said. He repeated that they knew I'd been helping the guerrillas. "Look," I said, "in the first place, I live by the side of the road. Anyone who comes to my house and says he's hungry, I feed him. Even if all I have is beans. That's how I was brought up, to feed the hungry who stop at my door. If one of you is hungry one day and comes to my house, I'll give you a plate of food."

He asked me about my husband, and again I told him I didn't know where he was. "I'm not in the habit of asking him where he goes when he leaves the house. I don't really care where he is, if you want to know." Then they asked, "Are you going to tell us you've never been to the union?" "That's right, I've never been to the union." "And you don't know who the head of the union was." "I know that," I said, "the head of the union was Bernardino Diaz Ochoa. They picked him up and killed him." "Who killed him?" "You, yourselves!" "Not me," one officer said. "Well, maybe it wasn't you, but it was another guard just like you. Because we never saw him again."

They used different kinds of approaches. Sometimes they used torture—they would beat me. Sometimes it was soft talk. I had to be careful not to contradict myself. Once they asked me how far I'd gotten in school, if I'd finished grade school or high school. I told them no, that we peasants never could go to school at all. When I was a child the nearest school was a three days' walk. I said I'd only been to second grade. "You aren't so dumb," the officer said. "You understand more than you let on. You know a lot more than you've told us." They asked about the "subversive activities" that took place in the union. "I don't know what you mean by subversive," I said. "Who is Sandino?" they asked. "Sandino," I said, "I never knew Sandino. I never even saw him."

When they came to rape me, after a while it was just...unbearable. I wasn't going to take it anymore and I told the officer, "What do your men think I am? A prostitute? Someone they picked up in some market place? I'm a married woman, and even if my husband and I are separated now, I have my children and they're all by him. And so do me a favour and tell your guards to leave me alone. Not to come near me anymore. I can't stand them." I was a prisoner but I think I made an impression on him because after that they just locked us all in that room and the guards didn't rape me anymore. But they'd already destroyed me. Raped me seventeen times. The first thing I asked for, later, when they let me go and I came to Managua, was to see a doctor. I didn't want to be pregnant,

I didn't want to have a baby by one of them. Even if it wasn't the baby's fault.

Toward the end, they said they were going to take me up in a helicopter and drop me from the sky. "Okay," I said, "I've never been in an airplane or a helicopter either. It's fine by me if I have to go up in one to die. If you are going to do it let's get it over with." But they didn't. Instead, they took the other prisoners and tortured them in front of me. They beat them. They burned them. They half-buried them in ant hills.

After six or seven days of that, they let me go. Four officers from Managua came with the papers ordering my release. They told me to bathe and wash my clothes. I had to wash my clothes and put them right back on again, wet. They gave me a comb for my hair because it looked like a bird had built its nest there. They gave me soap, powder, deodorant. Imagine, all of a sudden they were the "nice guys." After all they'd done to me! My belly was still black and blue, and I was in constant pain. I had bruises all over my body. They even had the nerve to ask if I wanted to stay there with them, to cook for them and things like that. "No thank you," I said, "I think I'll just go home."

All this time my husband was in the Soviet Union. By chance he found out I had been captured. He read about it in *Granma*,* there in the Soviet Union. Once he knew what was happening to me he couldn't go on studying so he asked to be sent home. As soon as he got to the Nicaraguan border they picked him up. That's when they told me I wasn't a peasant; I was the wife of a "subversive element." They tortured my husband terribly. They strung him up for nine days, they beat him to a pulp, and they left him for dead in an empty cell. And they tortured him psychologically too. They told him about me, how all of them had "had" me, and that I'd enjoyed it.

When finally we could be together again, I was afraid. I knew the kinds of things they'd said to him, that they'd tried to set him against me. I thought he was going to reject me, that he wouldn't be able to stand me anymore. But no.

* The Cuban Communist Party Central Committee's daily paper.

He told me, "Don't worry. That can happen to any woman who fights, or whose husband is involved in the struggle. Look at what happened to Doris Tijerino, and lots of other sisters, too. I don't know why you feel so ashamed." But I *did* feel ashamed, for everything I'd been through. It was terribly traumatic. I felt like I smelled bad, and I couldn't get rid of the smell. But my husband was understanding; he helped me a lot.

I think the peasant men did understand what their wives went through. At least all the ones I knew. The wives and husbands continued living together and afterwards they fought on with even more courage. The National Guard thought that by torturing people they would force us to abandon the struggle. They thought the peasants would go home and not take part anymore. It wasn't true. All that we suffered made us fight with more determination. When they burned houses—often with children inside—we fought all the harder.

It's been very hard on the children. Do you remember the case of the peasant woman named Maria Castil? She was captured along with her three children; they tortured her and then she disappeared. One of her kids was just six months old then, another was two and the other three. They're older now. Well, those children saw everything that was done to their mother. I was with them recently and they're completely traumatized.

My own daughter—the one who was fifteen months old when they picked me up—she's never gotten over her hatred of the Guard. I thought she was so young that it wouldn't affect her too much. But I was wrong. A few years later I took her to visit her father, who was in prison again. And right there, young as she was, she lashed out at the guards. She asked them why they were keeping her daddy. He hadn't done anything bad, she said. And she said to me, "Mommy, get some spinach for my daddy so he can get strong and break out of there with all his friends. Like Popeye..."

As for me, many women have suffered what I have. Think of the women in Cua, so many were captured, tortured and raped. There are many women in Nicaragua who can tell of the barbarities they've suffered. And many others who didn't live through the nightmares...After I was released I had to leave the country for a while. The Guard had left me in pretty bad shape. I went for medical treatment in the Soviet Union and was away for almost a year.

But when the fighting became more intense I came back to Managua, to Bello Horizonte. My kids were scattered among various relatives. We fought with whatever we had. We took everything they fired at us and sent it all right back to them: mortars and even bombs when they fell from the planes and didn't explode. We'd look for them, disarm them, fill them with fresh explosives and send them back where they came from. One day we even found a 500-pound bomb. We had a hard time digging it out because it made such a deep hole, but we managed to. We split it in half.

Peasant women attending an activity welcoming Cuban teachers, south of Esteli

One half was placed on the Bello Horizonte bridge, the other we sent somewhere else.

When the Front retreated to Masaya, we went with them. Later they told us the Guard was scared to go into the house where we'd been because they were afraid it was mined and would blow up. They discovered we weren't just a bunch of two-bit kids fighting with molotov cocktails or with *machetes* and stones as we'd done before. Most of us in that house were women, but we fought with everything we had.

You ask me about women in the struggle. In my case, my husband never tried to stop me. But my father did. He didn't like my being involved. He'd ask, "What are you fighting for?" He thought if you joined an organization, the next thing you knew you'd have "communism," That's what people were really afraid of, "communism." Of course people who *have* things are afraid of communism. Those of us who have nothing aren't afraid of it at all. Me, I say let it come!

My father always asked why *I* had to get mixed up in all this? For him, men were the only ones who were supposed to do anything at all. For example, men were the only ones who could study. That's why he never sent us to school. He said that one day we'd be married and have children and devote ourselves to our homes, so why did we need to know about anything else?

Now all that's different. We women have shown that we have a right to take part. Sometimes more right than the men. We proved ourselves during the insurrection. There were women who went off and fought without their parents ever suspecting what had happened, very young women too. Girls, really. We've always been discriminated against and now more than ever we're rebelling against the old roles. We want to fight. Sometimes we even have to fight our own husbands. Because there are times when husbands want us at home, confined within four walls, looking after the kids, feeding them, washing clothes, ironing and doing everything that has to be done in a house, without help from anyone.

We women have to organize ourselves, we have to join the women's association. We peasant women must organize ourselves, the domestic servants, too, all exploited women—organize themselves and work together to rebuild this wounded country and to fight for our own rights as women. . .

I'm living and working in Managua now. I'm still affected by the ordeal I went through but there's so much to be done. Our Organization of Democratic Women is going to join with the *Luisa Amanda Espinosa* Nicaraguan Women's Association. And the Socialist Party is going to unite with the FSLN to form a single party of the Nicaraguan working class.

When the war was over and we'd returned from Masaya, I found out that one of my sons had been killed, my oldest son, who was only seventeen. What's there to say? War is like that. You lose and you win, and sometimes you lose what you love the most. But what *really* upsets me is the way he died. If he'd been killed in battle, with a gun in his hand, maybe I wouldn't feel like I do.

A younger son of mine—who's nine now—and the seventeen-year-old were staying with my father-in-law. There were a number of people staying at the house. They discovered the Guard was nearby and since they didn't have enough weapons they decided to leave. Before fleeing, my son wanted to get some firewood so he could cook some food and leave it for the younger kids. He went for the wood and I guess they must have been watching the house. When he went out they followed him and that's when they got him. They shot him in the back. But he didn't go down right away. He ran into the hills and got as far as an empty house, where he closed himself in a room. But he was bleeding from the wound and groaning, so it was easy for them to find him—with the trail of blood and the moans and everything.

They followed him, dragged him out and brought him back to the woodpile where they'd shot him. They questioned him about his uncle, how many men his uncle had with him, etc. He wouldn't say a thing. His hair was long and real blond, and they asked him why he didn't get a haircut, if he was a pot smoker, and other stupid questions. He said no, he didn't smoke but he had his hair long because he wasn't going to cut it till the Revolution triumphed.

That's when they killed him. They killed my son, another comrade the same age, one of his little cousins who was five years old, another who was six months, and an older woman. A real slaughter. They dug a grave right there and buried three of them—the woman, the baby and my son. This summer I want to go up there and dig up his bones. I want to bring him back and bury him here or put him to rest in some cemetery nearby.

Four
Daisy Zamora

A woman and a man have just adopted a baby girl. It's a common event in Managua, like everywhere else. Yet this case is different from many others. The woman—in spite of wanting a daughter for years—failed to show up four times in a row for the necessary interview. "Work..." she told me, "and that sense one develops of not wanting to abandon the Revolution's problems to attend to something personal..."

Her face shows the intense emotion with which she approaches anything related to her child. She explains the circumstances surrounding her ambiguity. "Maybe it also had something to do with the times. My comrade and I talked about it a good deal. He would often say that perhaps this wasn't the best possible moment...that if we waited until things were better organized, I don't know...But he's always dreamed of a daughter, just as I have. And now that we have her, he's the first to get up with her at night, the first to pick her up and walk her...I wish you could see how this baby has changed our lives."

The woman is Daisy Zamora, Vice-Minister of Culture in the new National Reconstruction government. Her husband, Dionisio Marenco, is Minister of Domestic Commerce. And the baby, Maria Denise, is as old—or new—as the Revolution. Once fragile, abandoned and sickly, today she blossoms in her new home. Her new parents blossom with her.

We are with Daisy in her office. She is there every day,

94

*totally involved in the work of a ministry that didn't even
exist in the old Nicaragua. Her face is not easily forgotten:
prominent cheekbones, high forehead, large pale blue eyes
and very white skin. Her animated features transform
themselves along the whole range of expressions from total
seriousness to bright smile, but rarely touch on the extreme
of outright laughter. Her honey-coloured hair hangs loose
about her shoulders. Sometimes she pulls it back and up
into a small knot—"more comfortable for working."*

*Daisy, like the great majority of her comrades in the
struggle and now in reconstruction, is very young. She looks
even younger than she is. She's known as a poet—and a
very good one. As we begin our conversation, I stop for a
moment to look at her desk piled high with papers, projects,
plans, problems and solutions. I can't help thinking that
this woman with her tender but penetrating gaze must wish
at times to remove herself from the pressures of the
Revolution and hide in the seclusion of her poetry.*

DAISY: My family was well-off, but by the time I was born
they were on a downhill swing. My great-grandparents were
connected with the Zelaya government.* They were
Liberals. One of my great-uncles, Jose Dolores Gamez, was
an historian, and my great-grandfather was Zelaya's ambassador to Germany. When I was a child we lived with
my grandparents. My father was the oldest son, and he lived
with his wife and six children in his parents' house. That's
quite common in Latin America.

The whole world of bourgeois politics was an integral
part of my childhood. Everyone at home was a Liberal: it
was a family tradition. Mealtimes at my grandparents'
house were times of political discussion. Still, I can't say I
was particularly interested in politics then. I remember the
nuns at school did their best to discourage any concerns we
might have along those lines, except of course for activities

---

* Jose Santos Zelaya was president of Nicaragua from 1893 to 1909. A
member of the Liberal Party, his regime was characterized by the
national landowning bourgeoisie's rise to power.

which were acceptable in that society—hospital visits, the usual acts of charity...At that point I just went along with it all.

I do remember—it's like an ancient, very primitive memory—an incident that had a profound effect on my life. In 1954 there was an attempted coup against Somoza Garcia; it included Liberals, military men and so forth. My father and grandfather were involved, along with Lacayo Farfan, Fernando Aguero, the Baez Bone brothers, Pedro Joaquin Chamorro and others. They were discovered before they could carry out their plan. The repression came down hard and my father was taken prisoner.

We children were told he was on "a business trip." I wasn't even four years old. I remember opening the newspaper one day and there on the front page was a picture of the prisoners. I recognized my father immediately, but everyone insisted it wasn't him, only a man that looked like my father. I finally stopped asking, but I was convinced I was right. I began to be afraid at night, afraid to sleep with the lights off—and they tell me I started to bite people, though I don't remember. That was probably my earliest experience with a world that seemed terrifying. It threatened those I loved.

My grandfather had a great influence on my life. Somehow I never really identified with my parents. They had married young and were involved in all the customs of the petit bourgeoisie of the day. They flitted from social affair to social affair. They had their groups of friends and didn't take much interest in any of us. Maybe that's one of the reasons I leaned more toward my grandfather. He wasn't like that at all. He was very loving and patient and always had time for us. He was an interesting man, a renegade from the Liberal Party, someone who had rebelled against Somoza.

It was my great-aunt who raised me. She was my grandmother's sister and had moved into my grandfather's house when she became a widow. She was our auntie *par excellence*. She took care of all the little ones. When I went to live with my grandparents, at the age of three months, she took direct charge of me and raised me. Years later,

when she realized that my cousin and I were involved in the
struggle, she joined in and helped us out a lot. I don't think
she gave it much thought—she knew that Somoza was not a
just man, that repression was the order of the day, that
people were being murdered right and left...and she
wanted to fight against that...

I was a timid child. Even if I didn't have political
inclinations I did feel uncomfortable with the customs of
my social class. And since I never really took to the parties
and socializing, I began to be a lonely young woman. I took
refuge in reading. On weekends or when school was out I'd
go to my grandfather's farm with a pile of books. That was
my greatest joy. Reading awakened my need to write. I read
indiscriminately—anything I could get my hands on—and I
began writing a romantic type of poetry. Maybe that was
my way of trying to escape from my reality. The poems
were typically adolescent and pretty bad; I've destroyed
them all.

> Song of Hope*
>
> One day, the fields will stay green
> and the earth black, sweet and wet.
> Our children will grow tall on that earth
> and our children's children...
>
> And they'll be free as the mountain trees
> and birds.
>
> They'll wake each day, happy to be alive
> knowing the land was conquered once more, for them.
>
> One day...
>
> Now we plough dry fields
> each furrow wet with blood.

My life changed when I got to the university here in
Managua. I worked during the day and studied at night.
That was 1967. My poetry changed completely and I began

---

* All the poems in this chapter are by Daisy. This one was written in May
1967.

to write my first socially conscious lines. For me the period from 1967 to 1974 was one of searching, awakening to the pull of political commitments. It was also a time of fumbling. This fumbling was a product of my class origin. It made it impossible for me to commit myself completely to the struggle.

About the same time as I entered university I began to

Anita Gamez, Daisy's great-aunt

date the man who is now my husband, Dionisio Marenco
Nicho. He was just finishing his term as president of the
University Centre when I began my first year of general
studies. We met when I was elected to represent the first
year students at the Student Congress. That was my first
political involvement. I remember I wrote a few political
poems during that period.

But I still held back my involvement. I was very insecure
about my petit bourgeois background. And that made me
even more shy. Others of my age were more radicalized.
Most of them didn't have much patience with those of us
who hadn't reached their level. There were always political
activities on campus. I took part in a few strikes, but
nothing else. I followed what was going on during those
years but without really being able to take the leap and
involve myself completely.

By the time I finished my degree I had married Dionisio
and we had gone to live near Chinandega. He got a job at a
sugar mill and I followed him. I had told Dionisio to find
me a job and insisted that if I couldn't work I wasn't going.
I knew I'd go crazy if I didn't have work. When he first
went I stayed in Managua to finish my studies. I joined him
later, once he'd found me the job. I was teaching at a school
for the mill workers' children. I tried to make myself believe
that I was doing something worthwhile but deep down I
knew this wasn't what I should be doing.

I bought myself a bicycle and rode to school every day.
That alone was the talk of the town! Martha Zamora and
her husband lived there as well. Her husband was also an
engineer at the mill. Martha and I started a theatre group
among the kids at the school and put on several plays. It
may seem totally normal to you, but at that mill it was
completely scandalous for the wife of one of the engineers
to think of teaching the workers' children. Social classes
were rigidly defined. Engineers didn't mix with labourers.
The bosses lived in U.S. ranchstyle houses complete with
gardens. The workers' houses were wooden shacks on the
other side of town. The whole scene was hard for me to
take. But my response was to deal with it in an individual
way, as a teacher.

That was a difficult period for Dionisio and me. We were beginning to understand that we had political decisions to make that would affect every aspect of our lives, but we were still tied to certain family responsibilities. It wasn't yet possible for us to give up everything and dedicate ourselves completely to the struggle. Looking back, I think my husband hesitated in taking the leap because he was concerned about me. He didn't know if I would be able to give up my comforts and dedicate myself to the hard life of the Revolution. Then something happened that helped me make the decision. My grandfather became ill with cancer and I went to Managua. I stayed and cared for him for five months—until he died.

His death meant a break with the past for me. The most important person in my life had died. Throughout his illness, while I was nursing him, my grandfather tried to convince me that it was time I took a stand. He didn't say it directly, but I got the message. He'd say things like if he was young he'd have long since taken his jacket and rifle and gone to the mountains. He insinuated that I was letting him down, that he'd expected more of me. That was 1972.

For My Grandfather Vicente,
From January to His Death*

...Today I'm strong and your leaves
have left with January's wind.
Don't suffer though, I've seen new buds
among your branches.

The dry spell will pass and when May comes
your limbs will be covered with tender leaves.
And the rains will come again, and dry spells
     and winds...
But your sap is strong
you will have new buds
and your shadow, fresh as a willow
huge and bending
will live forever...

* Fragment, 1972.

Today the rain came back, the old rain.
The fields are green and the pathways rich with mud.
Everything as it was, but new and different,
the same and different.

Because it's the old rain that returns
like you who went and are here with me...

It was still going to take me over a year to really make the
break. I went back to the sugar mill and we continued
working and studying, searching, but not involving
ourselves directly in the struggle. Nevertheless, my
grandfather's illness and death were decisive for me.

In 1974 Roger Deshon, Juan Jose Ubeda and Roberto
Calderon—three members of the FSLN who were working
in Chinandega then—contacted my husband. He also had a
conversation with Tomas Borge. We discussed the
organization of a support cell for the Front. The discussions
we'd had as a couple began to extend to other politically
conscious people at the mill, technicians and professional
people who were also coming to realize that there had to be
a place for people like us in the revolutionary process. Some
of them said, "I don't know if I could stand that kind of
life. But we have to do something, we have to give
something to this struggle." It was a time of confusion as
we tried to find a place in the events that were developing
around us.

We organized a support network at the mill. It was a
fairly large network. We pledged money from our salaries.
We transported weapons and even purchased arms through
the mill. We helped in the transport of comrades. I worked
as a messenger and also served as a cover in the transport of
arms and comrades. But this work never really satisfied me.

Let Us Forget*

Let us forget
that this is the time for our cells to grow

* Written in 1974.

and separate and die and once again
(with millions of transparent leaves)
renovate themselves and fall,
perennial autumn, perennial spring.

Let us forget the words,
let us forget.
The grass on the trails, grows.

During that period we were also carrying out a clean-up
campaign at the mill, trying to put a stop to a whole series
of evils in the administration. Dionisio had brought in a
friend, Rigoberto Romero, and put him in charge of buying.
The mafia controlled the place and was protected by Irma
Guerrero—one of the region's local political bosses and a
Somoza faithful. All the lumberyards belonged to that
mafia. Rigoberto absolutely refused to accept bribes. That
got him into trouble—threats and worse. One day after work
they waited for Rigoberto on the highway and when he
came by they killed him. That was a breaking point for us.
It was totally clear that there was no alternative but armed
struggle. When you attempted to clean things up a bit, to
work honestly, right away you came up against the mafia,
the repression, the whole established scheme of things.

It soon became harder to work there. An informer must
have infiltrated the network or else had access to certain
information. The National Guard headquarters at the mill
began to be flooded with anonymous tips on our activities
and we had to lie low for a while. Once, for example, we
had planned an expropriation* of the mill's bank; we
needed the money for the Organization. We knew their
whole system, how they transported the cash, the roadways
leading out of the mill area, etc. and therefore thought it
would be a fairly easy operation. But just before we put our
plan into operation the National Guard commander
received an anonymous note revealing the whole plan and
denouncing Dionisio as its organizer. They called him in. Of
course he denied knowing anything about it. He said it must

* Bank robbery for political purposes.

be enemies he had in the area. They let him go but the
expropriation was cancelled.

Another time they sent in a list of mill employees involved
in the FSLN. It was absolutely accurate! But the National
Guard commander didn't believe it. He called my comrade
in again, showed him the list and said, "Just imagine. These
people are really something. Do they think we'd believe an
engineer is involved in this sort of thing!" He was totally
convinced it wasn't true. But at the end of 1975 the Guard
rounded up a lot of comrades in the zone. Juan Jose Ubeda
and Martha Cranshaw were arrested. Roberto Calderon
was captured in the mountains...and those of us in the
support cell just sat and waited for them to come and get us.
But the Guard never showed up.

We all stayed around for a couple of months without
really knowing what to do. It was impossible to continue
working at the mill. We decided to move back to Managua
and shortly after we arrived here we were contacted by the
FSLN. Dionisio continued to work as an engineer. I had a
job doing translations for a magazine called *Latinamerican
Thought*. I also did volunteer work mounting exhibitions
for Nicaraguan painters in the provinces. Oscar Perez
Cassar was the comrade responsible for our work with the
FSLN. He's dead now...Our work was mainly limited to
cover tasks: transports and errands. Our house became a
safehouse. There was an arsenal of weaponry stored in what
we called the "toy room." We also did support work for
several actions that took place around that time. We were in
the Insurrection tendency and it had developed a strategy
aimed at carrying out direct actions against the dictatorship
to accelerate its disintegration. That was when we started
planning for the attack on the National Palace.

One of our comrades had managed to bring a scanner into
the country. It enabled us to intercept all the Guard's radio
communications. They spoke in code but it was pretty easy
to break it. We soon understood everything they were
saying. Part of my job was sitting by that scanner listening
to everything the Guard said. We found out about their
operations before they carried them out—if, for example,
they were heading for one of our comrade's houses or if

they were about to set up roadblocks on the highway. Place "C," for instance, meant that they were going to block the highways and therefore that we couldn't transport arms that day.

Those were more or less my responsibilities—listening to the scanner, keeping a safehouse, hiding arms—all support tasks. I still felt dissatisfied with my level of participation. I began to feel a kind of discrimination. I talked about this with the other women but they didn't feel the way I did. I think this discrimination in the way tasks were assigned was less a result of my being a woman than because of my class background. Maybe they didn't trust me with other kinds of work and a more involved role.

I remember talking a lot about this with Dora Maria, confiding how hard it was for me to get over the inferiority I felt about my class background. I was clear about the role the petit bourgeoisie was called upon to play in the development of the revolutionary struggle. But I knew that that role didn't satisfy me. I wanted to be more involved, and on a different level. It wasn't until I left home completely, threw myself into the struggle full-time and went to fight alongside the other comrades, that I got over the feelings I had. I got over my insecurities by going to fight. . .

The planning and preparation for the National Palace operation was largely carried out by our cell. We spent a long time doing research and investigation. We obtained a detailed plan of the Palace, managed to get Guard uniforms, bought trucks, etc. Part of our investigation required gathering information on the comings and goings of the representatives who would become our hostages. We got photos of the most important ones so that members of the commando could instantly recognize those who were imperative to the action's success. For the week before the attack Dora Maria, Eden Pastor and Hugo Torres were based at my house. They studied each phase in minute detail—how they would enter the building, how the Guard was distributed, where the exit doors were located, etc. etc.

For the last few days before the operation half the commando stayed with us. You can imagine the difficulties of housing them! It was a large group, about sixteen in all, and almost everyone was taking part in this kind of operation for the first time. The comrades came to my house on a weekend, arriving one by one. We closed the house up as if we had gone away for the weekend. Because we didn't even have curtains on the windows, Dora and I lined them with paper. The comrades were distributed among three rooms. They couldn't move or talk much. We did have a bit of a food problem though. A few of us went to a nearby Chinese restaurant three times a day and bought take-out dinners. That might have appeared a bit unusual.

On the day of the attack—August 22, 1978—Dionisio was to call Dora Maria and confirm that everything was ready to go. Finally the coded message came: "Don Chinto is getting married at twelve o'clock." The comrades put on their uniforms and got ready. Right up to the very last minute the members of the commando didn't know what the action would be, only that it was an important one. When everyone was ready, they all filed out and sat down on a row of benches I had in the garden. We began the final instructions. We put up a map and Eden ("Don Chinto") explained the details of the manoeuvre. Files, complete with photos of the representatives, were passed out to everyone. We told them to remember the important ones— Luis Pallais, Irma Guerrero, Argenal Papi and the other people close to Somoza. It wasn't until then that the comrades fully understood the magnitude of the operation. I had a camera and it occurred to me to take pictures of all the comrades—while they were listening to the lecture, in their uniforms and ready to leave, climbing into the truck, etc. Unfortunately, these were later destroyed.

Shortly after the call, one of the comrades arrived with the truck. It was disguised as a Guard truck. I often think that if the Guard had been a little smarter they would have known that the truck was a fake. We had painted it at a movement garage and hadn't been able to get the right colour green. The truck was a little brighter than it should have been. Then there was the problem with the frame we'd built. When we threw the canvas over it and tried to tie it down we discovered that the frame was too high and there

was a space on either side between the bottom of the canvas
and the truck bed. All the comrades would be visible! I then
remembered that I had some boards in the "toy room."
Two of them turned out to be just the size we needed; we
nailed them into place and our truck was ready.

I was to give the order to move out. But just when I was
about to, our next-door neighbour decided to come out and
water her plants. Imagine! We didn't want any witnesses,
but the woman just wouldn't budge. Finally I had to give
the departure order anyway. Slowly, the truck pulled out. I
dashed back to the scanner hoping to follow the operation
through the Guard's communications. Dionisio was at work
and he later told me that he left the office around 11:30 and
went to the Plaza. He saw the truck drive up and park. The
comrades got out in perfect military formation and headed
toward the Palace. They passed through the enormous
doors without a slip. After the last comrade disappeared
inside Dionisio returned to work.

I stayed glued to the scanner. At first the Guard was
completely disoriented. They said, "There's a shoot out at
the Communications Palace." When I heard that I got
confused; I wondered if they'd been stopped along the way.
Coming from our house you pass the Communications
Palace before the National Palace. But the guard on the
radio had made a mistake. The shoot out was at the
National Palace. The next thing I heard was the guard
saying, "Careful, they're dressed like EEBI." That's when
I knew the commando had arrived safely.

    Commander Two*

    Dora Maria Tellez

                22 years old

    small and pale

    with her boots, her black beret

    her enemy uniform

                relaxed.

* Written in February 1979.

Behind the railing
I watch her talking to the comrades.
Beneath the beret her white neck
and the newly cut hair.
(Before she left we embrace each other.)

Dora Maria
the warrior girl
who blasted the tyrant's
heart.

The hardest part was reaching the Palace. Once we knew
the comrades were inside we all felt much better. We were
able to communicate with them by telephone from different
parts of the city. In fact, when the commando was on its
way out of the country, some of our comrades even went to
the airport to say goodbye. The operation was a total
success. The Guard never knew what hit them.

By September the time seemed ripe for the insurrection.
We had instructions to form a squadron from the same
support network that had functioned for the previous
actions. There were ten men and me in ours. Since I had
been training with them the whole time I insisted they
include me. It was absolutely imperative that I be involved.
I wanted to be fully integrated into the military work that
needed to be done.

The initial plan was for the thirteen squadrons to mount
simultaneous attacks on each of the city's thirteen police
stations and later regroup to carry out further actions. Our
squadron was scheduled to attack "Sierra One"—police
station number one—and from there move on to "South
Seven," where we would meet the comrades from Open 3
and San Judas. The attack was planned for September 9,
1978.

It wasn't decided whether or not I would go until the very
last minute when the final attack plan was being drawn up.
I had convinced Dionisio that I should be included—but it
had to be a collective decision. I told the comrades that I
was determined to go, that I had carried out all the tasks
assigned me, that I had shown sufficient discipline for this

kind of work, and that there wasn't any reason at all for them to exclude me. They agreed.

I was in the first car, the attack vehicle. There were four of us in the car. Another comrade and I had to jump out and cover the highway during the attack. There were eleven of us. Each was assigned a number from zero to ten. I was seven. We went into operation exactly at the time scheduled—6:00 p.m. All the assaults were to take place at the same time.

Something happened in the middle of the action that I'll never forget. Right after one of the commando members was wounded, an old man started waving a handkerchief at me. Imagine, there in the middle of all that fire he stood up to wave his handkerchief. I crossed over and took it and was able to bandage the comrade's arm. I'll never forget that gesture, that old man risking his life to help us.

The action was a success even though our preparation had been pretty rudimentary. Our plan was to destroy the station in ten minutes and in fact we were able to burn it to the ground in seven. But we did make a serious error in planning. We hadn't discovered that there was an EEBI barracks nearby. The guards came out of their barracks, crossed the highway and began to take their positions. The comrade in charge of our squadron told Dionisio to cover our retreat. He said we'd have to try to get to the nearby houses. Dionisio was firing from behind the car and I was trying to make my way out, moving from position to position.

At one point when the two of us were together, I asked Dionisio what he thought our chances of escape were. "Look," he said, "forget it. There's no way out of this. We're surrounded. I don't see how we can break the circle they've thrown around us. So be prepared to die." We calculated between 150 and 200 guards in all. So that's just what we did, prepared to die.

We tried to save as much ammunition as we could, defending our positions and waiting for the Guard to move in and finish us off. It was probably the other attacks that saved us. If ours had been an isolated action I don't think we could have escaped. But the Guard seemed disoriented.

We heard their commander ordering them to advance, but they didn't. We could hear gunfire over by San Judas—the attack spot nearest us—and we realized that battles were taking place in different parts of the city.

I don't know why, but suddenly there seemed to be a sort of truce. No shots were fired. Five of us moved toward a small rocky area. We thought we were the only survivors and decided our best move was to try joining up with the comrades over at San Judas. We made our way through a hilly area behind us. The trail was very difficult, practically straight up. We spent all night trying to get through. At one point we came close to some houses but a couple of dogs smelled us coming from a kilometre away and barked every time we moved closer. That was as far as we made it that night.

There was a beautiful moon over the hills. I cursed it being so bright. One of the Guard's helicopters passed overhead but they didn't see us. We were all exhausted. I volunteered for the first guard duty. I spent the whole night awake. At dawn I woke the rest of the comrades. I had an idea how we might get away. I suggested I go out to the highway. I thought that being a woman they might believe me if I said I had been caught in the middle of the previous night's battle. If that worked I might be able to get help.

We discussed my plan. The comrades claimed that it would be obvious I had taken part in the battle. We were all dressed the same, dark pants and shirts. And that wasn't as much of a problem as the blood I'd got all over my clothing from bandaging that comrade's arm. The blood, combined with the mud I'd picked up from crawling along the ground, made an awful mess. The others thought the plan too risky but I was firm in my decision. Dionisio said he wouldn't let me go alone, that he'd come with me. And that's what happened. We went together, pretending we were a couple who had been trapped in the cross-fire.

To Dionisio, Comrade*

Nearer ourselves than we ourselves
now.
More than when flooded with objects we moved
among those people
                    always outsiders.

We have nourished with life words
never spoken before.
Nothing said now, without sustenance.
No longer can I write you passive poems
shaded by locust trees and garden's willows.

I have no window now to look upon the sun
                    lighting gentians.
Our life is different today. That life
we always spoke about
and slowly came to live.

Now that we are ourselves
                    with thousands of brothers and sisters.

The two of us started out and right away the dogs began
barking. I refused to stop but continued going, right up to
the first house. Someone looked out and I made signs that
we needed help. The guy just told us to get out. The same
thing happened at the next house. The people went back
inside and closed the door. Dionisio thought it was too
dangerous to try more houses because someone was bound
to turn us in. But then I spotted a little house where a family
of caretakers lived. They were peasants who watched over
one of the estates. Dionisio called out to the old man. We
told him the story of our being trapped in the battle and he
said, "Sure friend, that was a terrible battle all right." He
brought us into his house. Those people did everything they
could for us, poor as they were. We told them we had some
friends who had also been caught. "Go and get them," they
said. Dionisio went for the others and I stayed at the house.
One of the young women—the old man's daughter-in-law

* Written in February 1979.

—came over and asked me what had happened. I could see that they didn't really believe our story but wanted to help us anyway. I think they already knew who we were. We were all scratched and covered with mud. I told her the truth, that we were the ones in the battle and that we needed their help. I asked her to let me wash and lend me a change of clothing so I could get to the highway and look for help. The poor woman began to cry and said of course she would help. She and another young girl got out their best things. They gave me a yellow blouse, a pair of tan pants, and red tennis shoes. They combed my hair and lent me an orange scarf. And they brought me a cup of coffee. I cried. Every time I think of those people I cry. They risked their lives to help us. They even washed my feet.

When the rest of the comrades arrived, I was totally transformed! Again I insisted on going to the highway. Because of my physcial appearance, we thought I might be able to pass for a foreigner. But Dionisio kept saying he didn't want me to go alone. After much discussion we decided that another comrade, who had blond hair and blue eyes and could also pass for a foreigner, should go with me. One of the sons of the peasant family took us as far as one of the nearby estates. From there we made our way to the highway. There were guards all over the place. We just braced ourselves and walked right past them, me speaking English and my comrade answering in German. We made it to the home of one of our supporters and he was able to rescue the others.

I had arranged with my fifteen-year-old sister that if I was in trouble I would call home using a false name. I called my parents' house at 6:30 that morning and managed to let my mother know where I was. She and one of my brothers came to pick me up. That began a series of clandestine comings and goings. We had to find places to hide, something each of us was supposed to deal with on our own. We had agreed to use my mother as a check-point for making contact among ourselves but that proved impossible. The Guard arrived at her house and arrested my mom and one of my brothers.

My mother withstood it all very well. She was very brave.

My brothers and sisters told me that when the Guard came to get her she never for a moment let on that she knew who they were looking for. They held her at the police station for eight days, and my brother for 45. Though they didn't physically torture her, they mistreated her psychologically. And she passed the test with flying colours. My brother, too. Neither of them were members of the FSLN, but of course they were against the regime. They had helped us in all sorts of ways and when the time came to confront the repression they showed they were capable of holding up.

Meanwhile, we were going from house to house seeking refuge. Some people we knew were willing to hide us for a few days, others weren't. The Guard had launched a nationwide repressive operation. Managua was being searched practically house by house, so it was impossible for legal cadre like ourselves to go underground. We were told to seek asylum in an embassy. We went to the Honduran Embassy, the only one that wasn't surrounded by guards. They granted us asylum. We spent a month there, until we were able to get safe conduct permits. We reached Honduras safely and began to work in the rearguard there.

Once out of the country I was again reduced to operational work. And again I felt dissatisfied with it. I was stationed in Panama and then in San Jose, Costa Rica. There were plans to open an underground hospital in San Jose and I received instructions to organize it with Jacobo Marcos. We got the hospital set up, taking care of details ranging from scrounging beds from the Red Cross to co-ordinating surgical teams. Then, when the wounded comrades from the Southern Front began coming in, we organized political classes for them.

To Comrade Blas Real Espinales*

I met Salvador (that was his war name)
in exile in Honduras. He came with Laura
to the house where I saw him only once.
He was thin. With strangely sweet and luminous eyes.

* Written in December 1978.

(The following week he went back to Nicaragua
where he died in battle in Chinandega.)
I barely knew him
                        but keep on seeing
those eyes, intensely open and vulnerable
                                        to death.

Women's involvement in our struggle has become greater
and more intense. I often rediscover childhood friends when
I least expect to. That's what happened with Nora Astorga.
We had known each other as children. Later, after Dionisio
and I returned to Managua from the sugar mill, I ran into
her at the university. We found out later that we had both
been members of the Organization, but since neither of us
could be sure exactly where the other stood we simply didn't
say anything.

Nora was a key person in the Perez Vega action.* She
was the one who lured Vega to the house where the
comrades executed him. Dionisio and I were involved in
support work for that action. Some of the comrades stayed
at our house. I remember Dionisio telling me on the night of
the action that the comrades had mentioned that a young
bourgeois woman, a member of the Organization, had taken
part. I asked who she was but he said they hadn't told him
her name. I had a hunch it was Nora.

The next morning when the first news flashes referred to
a "Mrs. Nora Astorga" I knew I had been right. I tried to
find out if she was all right and was told she was already out
of the country—everything had gone as planned. Much
later, I ran into Nora in Costa Rica. One of my first tasks in
San Jose was obtaining false papers for the Nicaraguan
comrades. I took Nora to Immigration where she was
legalized under a new name. That's when we had a chance
to talk once again, this time more freely...

My last job before the July 19 victory was at Radio
Sandino. Radio Sandino was a joint project of the three
tendencies. At first I was in charge of programming and

* For Nora Astorga's account of this action see Chapter Five.

also worked as an announcer. Later a professional announcer came to work with us and I just handled the technical aspects of programming. One of the programs we developed was "The Sandinist Woman." Our goal was to raise consciousness around women's participation in our struggle. We talked about women's involvement in all aspects of the Revolution and about how many women had given their lives for liberation, women like Conchita Alday, Arlen Siu, Luisa Amanda Espinosa, and many others.

When the war ended and I returned to Managua one of the first things I did was visit the peasant family that had taken us in that night. They were happy to see me and gave me a huge sack of delicious green mangos. But the young woman who had helped me change clothes wasn't there. I met her later in Jinotepe where I was speaking at a special tribute for Arlen Siu. I was very nervous about speaking in public since up till then I'd only spoken for Radio Sandino. When my talk was over I saw a woman coming toward the stage from out of the crowd. She was saying, "It's her...It's her..." At first I didn't know who she was. "Don't you remember me?" she asked. "You came to my house one night and I gave you clothing..." Then I recognized her. We were chatting away when she asked if I would take my sunglasses off. Turning to her mother, who had caught up with her by this time, she said, "See, mama, I told you, look how pretty her eyes are." She gave me a big hug and asked if we'd all managed to come out all right. "We're all alive," I told her.

Five

Nora Astorga—One March 8

March 8, 1978 had a special impact in Nicaragua. "Dog" Perez Vega, a particularly brutal general in the National Guard, was executed by members of the Sandinist National Liberation Front. Local and international news services immediately linked the name of a woman—Nora Astorga— to the action. "She invited him to her house," reported the media, "and several hours later, he was found there, dead." Nora Astorga had scored an important victory in the struggle against the Somoza dictatorship and, in particular, for her sisters on International Women's Day.

After the execution she wasn't heard from again. She was able to elude the intensive dragnet set up by the National Guard. Today, in the new Nicaragua, Nora Astorga is still a member of the FSLN. She is also a lawyer and the mother of four children. Her title is Special Attorney General. She is in charge of bringing to justice the more than 7,500 ex-guards and other functionaries of the Somoza regime who are being tried for their crimes in the people's courts.

Who is Nora Astorga?

We went to the house which is temporarily being used as the Special Courts office. The office was filled with dozens of young people, all involved in preparing trials for those who for so many years have abused and tortured this nation. We told the receptionist that we wanted to see the Attorney General. Our appointment was set for two days later.

Nora received us in her small, almost barren office. We talked for a long time. She has the ability to speak about her involvement in the struggle in Nicaragua with an uncommon fluidity and orderliness. Perhaps her training as a lawyer is responsible for her ease with language. She speaks intimately about her life, but what she says relates to many women of her class and culture. Her sensitivity comes through at all times. Nora is a woman who has done something which, by its nature, will always seem somewhat startling. Yet she is a woman like many others, with a history of growth, blows, small triumphs and limitations. She is a comrade who has matured through confronting the problems of class, sex and commitment.

But I want to let her speak for herself.

NORA: I was born 31 years ago and am the oldest of four brothers and sisters. My family is petit bourgeois. My father was a cattleman, my mother a housewife. My father had an important influence on my life. From the time I was a child he kept telling me that I was an individual who could study and become whatever I liked. He didn't want me to become a housewife who had learned only to cook and sew—which was the usual education in my day. He convinced me that being a woman was simply a descriptive characteristic, not a limitation. His pushing me to develop myself was not uncommon among Latin American families of our class. Often fathers would encourage their first child, of either sex, to pursue their unrealized ambitions.

I had some social consciousness even as a child. I always felt privileged. The fact that I had every comfort in life made me feel obliged to give to others. To begin with, this took the form of charity. It was acceptable to do the type of so-called social work promoted through the religious schools—going to poor neighbourhoods and giving talks on hygiene and religion, or going once a week to a hospital to visit sick children or to an old-age home to visit the aged. These were called "good deeds." Little by little I began to realize that charity wasn't enough. Of course, I didn't have a political analysis at that point but I was beginning to understand that something more than charity was needed to change people's basic living conditions.

Then started my political development. My first political experience was during the 1967 election when Aguero* ran against Somoza. Aguero seemed to be a positive alternative to Somoza so I worked for his election. My parents' response to my involvement was to get me out of the country. They sent me to study in the United States—in Washington, D.C.—and didn't let me return until they thought I had "forgotten all my crazy ideas." That was during the summer of 1969. In September I entered the university here to study law. I still had a naive belief in the

---

* Fernando Aguero was an opposition candidate in 1967. He later sold out to the National Guard.

idea of justice in Nicaragua and, consequently, entered law school with a lot of illusions. I couldn't have known the atrocities which passed for justice.

Toward the end of that year a comrade from the FSLN came and talked to me. He made me question who I was, what I was doing and what I had the ability and obligation to do. That's how I began my first timid collaboration with the FSLN. They never tried to force me to do anything beyond my real capacity. They would give me things to read and let me form my own conclusions, guiding me along. I started to really identify with Sandinism and to understand that this was where I could and should put my energies.

Those were years of intense student struggles. I became secretary of the Student Centre at the Catholic University. A lot of our work related to political prisoners. I was also beginning to do some support work with the FSLN. I let my house be used for meetings, served as a messenger, transported comrades from one place to another—things like that.

The comrade from the FSLN that I worked most closely with was Oscar Turcios. He taught me what working with the FSLN was all about. He taught me about the dedication I would need if I were to join. But at the same time as he encouraged me, and other beginners, to move closer to the Organization, he also seemed to understand our limitations. He was enormously patient with us. Without wanting to idealize him—he had his faults like anyone else—I'll always remember Oscar with a great deal of love.

I kept working like that for a while, collaborating but on the periphery. Then when the FSLN split into three tendencies my participation diminished quite a bit and I became isolated from the political struggle. I didn't want to take sides in the split so my involvement was reduced almost exclusively to giving financial aid to the tendencies. . . But to be completely honest, there were personal reasons as well for my poor showing at that time.

I had married in 1970, a year after beginning to collaborate with the FSLN. At the time, my husband was the student representative to the FSLN from the National University; supposedly he was at a higher level of political development than me. He was a pre-militant* and I was only a collaborator. When we decided to get married I told him that I didn't want anything to get in the way of my political life. "O.K., we'll be married," I told him, "but my political life comes first." He agreed, in principle, but it didn't work out that way in practice. That was one of the reasons for my falling back politically during that period.

My marriage lasted for five years. It was an unhealthy, destructive type of relationship. Can you understand that kind of conflict, where personal problems get a stranglehold on your life? You have lots of good intentions but the way you lead your life doesn't allow you to act on them. It wasn't until I made a complete break with that relationship that I was really able to devote myself to the struggle.

When I first left my husband I thought the world was going to fall apart. But the experience forced me to ask myself the political questions I'd posed back in 1969. Was I really doing everything I could, or was I just fooling myself, participating only to the extent that I didn't have to admit to myself that I wasn't doing anything? I had to face my own situation, as a woman, a professional person, and as a political being. Of course, the answer was clear. I decided: no more excuses. I had to move ahead, become more involved. So I made the leap, and in March 1978 the opportunity arose for me to carry out the action you know about.

Before talking about the Perez Vega operation itself, I should go back a bit and give you some background. At the time, I was working as the lawyer and head of personnel for one of Nicaragua's largest construction companies. The job gave me a very good cover. It allowed me to move in government circles. I had contact with ministers of state and, to a certain extent, with members of the National Guard. Although the company I worked for didn't have direct contracts with the Guard, a situation developed that

---

* A term used by the FSLN to describe a comrade who will soon be eligible for full membership in the organization.

made it possible for me to get close to Perez Vega, a general in the National Guard. He had some land near one of the projects our company was building and was interested in having it developed. That's how I first got to know him.

After Vega and I met, I informed the Organization about our working relationship. I told them I was in a good position to get closer to the "Dog." We knew we could take advantage of the situation to get information from the guy. The comrades told me to keep the work relationship going but not to push it any further for the moment.

The situation stayed like that for just over a year. When I had to go to see him at his office I would play my role to the letter—cordial and cool at one and the same time. Being pleasant to that man was one of the most difficult parts of the whole thing. The guy was famous for being a womanizer. He was a classic cop, known for being able to have any woman, how, where and whenever he pleased. He'd use persuasion to get what he wanted. And if that didn't work he'd use force. And in his role as general he was the worst sort of animal you could imagine. He was a torturer—the worst kind. Any adjective I could use to describe him would be pale in comparison to the reality of his crimes.

I had to be very careful in how I dealt with him. When my divorce came through he thought I would be easy prey. He began an all-out campaign to get me into bed. That's when I told my contact in the Organization that this was a good time to get what we wanted out of the guy. He told me to keep Vega interested and they'd get back to me.

I felt as if I was walking a tightrope most of the time. I had to keep him thinking I would give in and at the same time had to hold back until the time was right. Maybe it was my ambivalence that kept him interested. But the situation got to the point where it was impossible to keep him dangling any longer. Either I had to give in or we'd lose our chance. He'd say, "It's now or never." I remember my last excuse. "Look," I told him, "you know I'm interested but it's going to have to be when I want. I'm not the kind of woman you're used to. I'm an independent woman and I have the right to choose the terms." He accepted that, for the moment. A short time later, the comrades had the plan ready. Originally the plan was to kidnap Vega and exchange him for comrades that were in jail.

My contacts in the Organization were very straight with me. They told me what going through with the action would mean for my life, and for my children. They explained that I would bear the brunt of all kinds of misconceptions and suspicions about what I had done. My participation in this action, they said, could mean my giving up everything. They told me to take the time I needed before making a final decision.

I thought over the whole thing again and again. I had two daughters then—one was two years old, and the other six—and I was terribly attached to them both. I finally decided to go ahead with it. It may seem ironic, but part of my decision was precisely because of my children. I believed that by doing my part I would be helping to bring about a better world for them, and other children like them. It was hard for me to think about being separated from my girls, but I made the decision calmly. It was something I felt I had to do—wanted to do. The decision was a mature one, made without idealism. I said to the comrade, "O.K., I'm willing."

The plan was for me to get him over to my house on March 8. Three comrades would be there, waiting. One was to hide in a large closet off the master bedroom, another in the room across the hall and another in a smaller room. I was to disarm him without arousing his suspicion, get him in a defenseless position, then grab him and give the signal—a code word—for the comrades to spring into action.

On the day of the action I called Vega at four in the afternoon. He wasn't in—they said he was up North or something—but the plan couldn't wait. I left a message with his secretary. "Just tell the General," I said, "that something he's been very interested in for a long time can happen tonight. And if it doesn't happen tonight I can't guarantee that it ever will. Tell him I'm waiting for him at my house."

Within 45 minutes he called to say he'd be right over. I

had only a few minutes to get ready. I dashed out to the supermarket to get some liquor and a couple of rolls of film. I didn't have anything in the house. About fifteen minutes after I got back, the General showed up. I laugh when I think of it now...even then it seemed a bit funny to me. Of course I wasn't laughing at the time, but his approach did surprise me. He came immediately to get what he'd been after for so long. And once he got to my place he didn't use any of the subtleties men sometimes do. No small talk, no "let's have a drink," nothing. He came in and said, "Here I am, let's go." I asked if he didn't want a drink first but he said, "No, no, what for?" And that's how it began—we went right to the bedroom.

Things went exactly as planned. I disarmed him, then got him undressed. At just the right moment I gave the signal and the armed comrades burst in. Vega put up a good deal of resistance. He was a very strong man. He began shouting for his bodyguard, who didn't hear him. I think he was listening to the car radio and had all the windows rolled up.

In order not to have to kill the driver, the comrades told me to go out and get him to leave. I went downstairs and told him the General wanted him to go and buy a bottle of Plata rum. Vega kept a lot of liquor in the car, a variety of high-class brands, but I knew he wasn't likely to have Plata. It's a working class brand and he was too elegant for that. The driver said, "The General wants *that*?" "Yes," I told him, "the General says for you to get it, and fast. You know he doesn't like to be kept waiting." "O.K., O.K.," he said. And he left.

That was when the "Dog" was executed. I got the car and brought it around. The comrades came out with the weapons. They had killed him while I was getting the car. He put up too heavy a fight and they had to do it. Looking back, I think it was better that way. The guy was a torturer. I don't even know if he could be considered a human being.

Sometimes when I think about the experience I think that I had the upper hand through it all. I had the backing of an organization and was carrying out a carefully worked-out plan. But then I realize what he might have done to me, what he undoubtedly had done to dozens of young women he'd taken advantage of because they needed money or a favour of some kind—maybe they had a relative in prison or something like that. He was renowned for that kind of thing—getting women to give themselves to him in return for favours of one kind or another.

In any case, I brought the car around, we got in and I took the comrades to where they were being picked up by someone else. I returned the car to the person who had lent it to me—who, needless to say, didn't know what it had been used for. Then I went to meet the comrades who were waiting to get me out of the city. Everything went as planned.

I went underground. I was on the Northern Front for a while taking military training. Later they got me out of the country. I returned to fight on the Southern Front in June 1978—three months after Vega's execution. I was political leader of four squadrons. That was my first real military experience.

But to go back a bit. I left my children at the home of a cousin of mine shortly before the Perez Vega action. My cousin was married to a North American and I thought it would be a safe place for them during the repression which would likely immediately follow the action. After a short time at my cousin's the children went to live with my mother.

Through various comrades I was able to find out how my children were doing and that they were well. What I didn't know for some time was how hard my parents took my involvement in the action. It was a blow they hadn't expected. How could they have? Their initial response was practically to disown me. It took a long time before they could even attempt to understand what I had done. But in time they did understand although it hasn't been easy for them.

It has been hard on the children as well. The older one resented the fact that I didn't tell her I was leaving. She was just six, but even at that age... When I saw her again, a year later, the first thing she said to me was, "One day you were home and the next day you'd gone. You never told me where. You didn't even write to me...You abandoned me." She'd often say, "If you had just told me that you had to go away I might have understood. But what I couldn't stand was that you never told me anything." She's very mature for her age, maybe because she's been through things many other kids haven't.

During the preparation for the Perez Vega operation I got to know another member of the Organization who is now my husband. He is the comrade who got me out of Managua after the execution. Later, in spite of the limitations of underground life, we had the opportunity of getting to know each other better. We fought together on the Southern Front. In fact, he was squadron leader in my first battle.

My relationship with this man has been very good. As far as I'm concerned he's close to perfect. He's an excellent comrade, very honest and understanding—a real revolutionary. As you can imagine, we haven't had that much time together but what we've shared has been profound. When we were together in the mountains we became very close. In that kind of struggle time takes on new dimensions. When people are able to be together in conditions like that, they tend to live with an intensity that's unusual in more normal times.

It was an interesting experience being a woman on the Southern Front. All of a sudden you weren't a lawyer or a professional—in most cases you weren't even thought of as a woman or a man—you were simply one comrade among many. Most of us, particularly the women, had never had that experience before. I think women were accepted and appreciated as comrades by everyone. In training, the same was expected from us as from the men. And yet, in the normal everyday tasks—hauling water, for example—the men always helped. And it wasn't a matter of looking down on our being women. I was pregnant during that time and I remember the comrades always trying to help me so I wouldn't have to lift heavy weights. Things like that.

When I was six months pregnant I was told I'd have to leave the guerrilla camp and go back to the city. I didn't

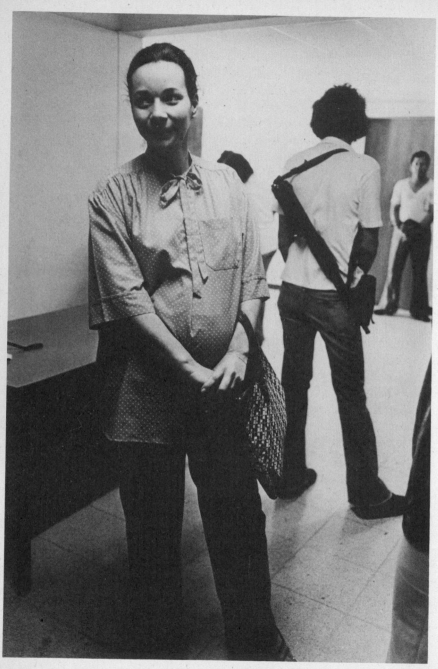

Nora at the makeshift court building the day the first counter-revolutionary was sentenced

want to. I thought I was still in shape to be in the mountains, but the comrades though otherwise. "You can't let your personal feelings get in the way of life here for the rest of the fighters," they told me. "You are too far along for us to feel comfortable about your being here." So they sent me to the city. I was put in charge of finances for the Southern Front and of supplies in general.

I've had three different jobs since July 19. I was Assistant Attorney General for a week. The national FSLN leadership appointed me to the job while I was still in the army. Then I was put in charge of the army's finances. We had to start from scratch and set up the system. At first I knew almost nothing about financial systems, but I had an excellent group of comrades to work with. I was at that job through October, and then—responding to another directive—I took this job. It's not easy. Here in Nicaragua there never was what you might call official justice. We've had to put together a legal system from almost nothing. It's an important and difficult political task. We have a fine group of people working together on the project and we're confident we'll be able to handle the job.

Nicaraguan women have never been apathetic. In spite of the fact that we haven't always participated in the front lines, we were always concerned about what was going on. And there is another thing: women here love their children with a passion. They love their children and the people in general. Our women are very demonstrative, very committed, and once they're involved they begin to grow.

I worked with Lea Guido, Gloria Carrion and others organizing AMPRONAC. I remember how the women were shy at first. They'd tell us, "O.K., I'm willing to work in my neighbourhood, but just for water and electricity and things like that. . ." But with a bit more work—we didn't have to make such an enormous effort—those women began taking part on an ever more solid basis. And, as a matter of fact, we had a very strong group of people there. These women saw what was going on in their lives and they wanted to confront and change things.

You ask me if I think there has been any backsliding in terms of women's involvement. Maybe in some sectors. For example, maybe there are bourgeois women who are saying, "I've done my part. Now it's time to take a rest for awhile." But not many working class or peasant women. You won't find any backsliding among those women who suffered the repression head-on. There is too much at stake.

In fact, I think our working class men are more traditional than the women. Maybe it's just my personal opinion but it seems to me that our women are stronger. They're the ones who have had to earn the family's living in most cases. Our women have had to work to support families just like the men. And that's on top of their other tasks as housewives—that whole second shift of domestic work. *That* is something that we haven't been able to change yet. Women have to attend to their husbands and children in addition to whatever work they do outside the home. In other words, they're supposed to be superwomen. This is something that hasn't changed that much even for those of us within the Organization. It's beginning to change but it's not yet a radical change.

Nicaraguan women have taken part in the revolutionary struggle and that experience has had a profound effect on us. Women won't be apathetic again. We won't ever again let ourselves be isolated from society. Some might withdraw momentarily for some reason, but I'm positive that sooner or later they'll be back in the swing of things. And with renewed strength. We see this in our women's association— those women are tremendous fighters. Women were of crucial importance in the insurrectional struggle and we know that we—who are 51 per cent of the population—are vital to our country's—and our own—development today.

Six

The Women in Olive Green

Lovely girl of the FSLN
with your boots and pants of drill
machine gun in hand
your long flowing hair
that grew in the month of April.

You left your lover
to begin another relation
for your true love
is not he but another
it's the love of an entire nation.*

I joined the Sandinistas when I was fourteen years old. My involvement grew out of the poverty so many of us suffered. While I was still in grammar school I began to notice the contradictions in all the areas of our lives—in the countryside, in production, in the economy, in education. Oh, I couldn't analyze it like that then, but I felt it all right. And then there were the assassinations. By 1973 the number of comrades being killed was increasing dramatically. Their deaths had an impact on us; they convinced us that we had to take up arms.

So for me, joining the Front was a logical consequence of everything happening around me.

* First verse of the song "Girl of the Sandinist Front," words and music by Carlos Mejia Godoy.

129

This is Ana Julia Guido, a young woman with an honest face and strong body. She is dressed in olive green and carries a heavy pistol at her hip. The rolled-up sleeves of her army shirt reveal traces of the notorious "mountain leprosy" that was so common among guerrillas assigned for long periods to the mountains. Ana Julia works in Personal Security, the office responsible for the bodyguards of the Revolution's leaders.

Like so many of her sisters, Ana Julia speaks about her life and experiences with simplicity. In Chapter Two, we heard the testimony of three comrades who made the rank of commander, extraordinary human beings—people who would have stood out no matter what their sex or task. In this chapter we will hear from rank-and-file women soldiers. Theirs is an experience that is common to women in Nicaragua. Many young women, from the countryside and cities, decided that the logical way to participate in the struggle was to join the people's troops. And like Ana Julia, most of these women have stayed in the Sandinist People's Army.

ANA JULIA: I'm from Matagalpa, in the northern part of the country. My mother is a peasant. My father also works in agriculture; he supervises work on the ranches. There were six of us kids. Two died in the war. My 20-year-old brother was killed on July 19, the day of the victory. Another brother died two years earlier. He was only seventeen. I only completed my first year of junior high school. Then I joined the Sandinistas. My father worked in the fields then and had direct contact with the Sandinist guerrillas working in the area. Many of the comrades came to the house to see him. That's how I met them...

When I first joined, I was "legal." I worked in the neighbourhoods and had jobs such as buying clothing, food and other supplies for the guerrillas. I also acted as a messenger. Later I took part in an assault on a bank and had to go underground. We describe it as being "burned." I was publicly identified as a member of the FSLN and would have been in great danger had I remained at home.

Ana Julia Guido

When I went underground I was sent to a training school in the mountains. It was given by Tomas Borge. We studied political, military and cultural questions. We also learned some basic nursing techniques. But the emphasis was on military training. Monica Baltodano and I were the only women. It's because of those classes that I'm the guerrilla I am today. Eight or nine of us decided to form a group in the mountains. The others all went to work in mass organizing, in the neighbourhoods, or in the underground student movement.

I was in the mountains for two-and-a-half years. At first I was the only woman. Later on, several more came. But it was never difficult being a woman there, not at all. The things that people gossip about when they think of women and men together in the guerrilla just aren't true. There was never any lack of respect on the part of our male comrades. On the contrary, there was an incredible solidarity.

Maybe the experience in the mountains never seemed that hard to me because I was psychologically prepared. Probably the hardest thing was building up your physical resistance. It takes about six months before you get used to the rains, the hunger and the long hikes. The hikes were the hardest part—going days and days with only a little food. And the food didn't fill or nourish you. Usually it was pure carbohydrates. And then there was the monkey meat, which *is* nourishing. . . But I gradually got used to living outdoors and in the mountains.

I was involved in my first battle soon after I got to the mountains. You're always afraid in the first one. I had never even heard gunfire before. When it begins, you feel a kind of desperation, but then you calm down and begin to identify the shots. The comrades always help a lot. By the next battle it all seems normal. In fact, they say the second is the most dangerous one because you're likely to get over-confident.

In 1977 during the battle in which Commander Carlos Aguero was killed, Ana Julia's column was reduced to thirteen comrades. Right after, the column divided into two. Ana Julia and five others covered the retreat of the other seven. Ana Julia's group was captured and taken to Santa Rose for interrogation. Later they were transferred to Waslala where Ana Julia spent three months in jail. After that, she suffered through another six months in prison in Puerto Cabezas.

When she got out, Ana Julia went back to Matagalpa to take part in the August 1978 insurrection. Several months later, during the last weeks of the war, she was named head of the rearguard coming in from Honduras, an area including part of the departments of Leon, Chinandega and Esteli.

ANA JULIA: I always gave orders in as comradely a way as possible. I tried to make sure that people understood exactly what was required. Occasionally I noticed that someone was sulking because a woman had given him an order. It was never direct but I could sense it. When the situation arose I had to talk to the man about his attitude. It was necessary for him to realize that we women had earned our right to participate in the struggle. I'd explain that we deserved our rank and he'd have to understand that. There weren't too many of these problems though and the ones that did arise were not severe.

Participating in the struggle has changed my life tremendously. If I had stayed at home who knows where I'd be now. I know now that I'll devote my whole life to the Revolution. I'm prepared for anything, to go wherever they need me most. If I had stayed at home, I'm sure I wouldn't feel this way.

It's not that I don't have any personal ambitions. I do. I'm going to be 21 soon and what I want more than anything is to have a baby. I've been thinking about it since I was about eighteen. And especially now—so many comrades in the Organization have children. Now that they're home again, they can sit down with their children and tell them about their experiences. It's great to watch. My comrade was killed in the war but I still think a lot about my desire to have children. And also to study. If the Organization were to ask me what I wanted to do, I'd say I want to study. But if they need me here then here I am.

We met Marlene Chavarria Ruis in a town near the northern border called Ocotal. Marlene is currently working in the communications division of the army's General Staff in the area. We talked with this nineteen-year-old combatant in the garden outside her office. The house that serves as her office was once the home of a wealthy American. Now the house and the surrounding land is used by the people. Marlene is better known by her war name—Yaosca.

YAOSCA: I only finished my first year of high school because that was when I joined the FSLN. It was in January

Yaosca

1977. I was living in Santa Cruz at the time. My uncle was the first one of us to work with the Organization. It was through him that I made my first contact. I was made messenger for the whole zone. I carried correspondence and sometimes oral messages. After a while it became too dangerous for me to work legally and I had to go underground.

At first I didn't tell my parents that I was going underground. I'm the oldest of eight children, the one who had a chance to study and the one who took care of the house. So even though my parents are Sandinistas they wouldn't have wanted me to leave home. I told them that I was going to Leon to study and work, that I couldn't stay in Santa Cruz because the Guard was already looking for me. But instead of going to Leon I went underground. Three days later my parents found out what had happened. I sent them a letter asking them to understand why I hadn't been able to say goodbye. I knew they wouldn't have let me leave but I had made up my mind and no one was going to stop me.

For the first six months I worked as a messenger between Esteli and Jinotega. Then I went to the mountains. I didn't find it that hard. There was the cold, the mosquitoes and all, but when you looked at your comrades and saw they were all suffering through the same things, that you were all struggling together, you didn't mind it. Actually, I was very happy there.

As soon as I arrived at Omar Cabeza's camp they started me on military training. From the beginning I did well—I never had any problems with the hikes or anything else. Peasant women always have a good deal of resistance. The hardest part was the obstacle course. You had to run very quickly, without stopping, along a very narrow log. Many comrades would fall off. I used to slip but always managed to straighten up and keep going. They used to time us. Lucio started off better than anyone else, with Alfonsito in second place. I caught up with Alfonsito and in the end I passed him and took second place.

For the first month I was the only woman, although there were women at the other camps further into the mountains. The comrades were very nice to me—some said they spoiled me because I was the only woman, but that's not true. They treated me the same as everyone else. About a month after I got there three other women arrived.

I fell in love with a comrade at the camp and we decided to get married. Everything was fine. At my wedding all the comrades lined up in close formation. Then the commander said, "Comrade Yaosca and Comrade Justo are man and wife," and he asked the others to respect us. Whenever there was a wedding or it was someone's birthday we'd have a party; we'd sing and sometimes even have a drink. Sometimes we'd make rice pudding or get hold of a can of sardines which we'd all share.

Part of our work in the mountains involved gaining the confidence and support of the peasants. The National Guard had convinced many of them that we were rapists and murderers. They were afraid when they first saw us, all the more so because we were armed. We had to work hard to convince them we were friends. Sometimes we'd have to use extreme tactics. When we'd enter a village we'd surround the huts and tell people we were from the Guard. We'd call them out and then begin to talk to them. They trembled when they looked at us. We'd tell them that we weren't the Guard, that we were the FSLN and were fighting so they could have a better life. We talked with them about the exploitation that they themselves experienced. It was nothing new to them. They lived it. We told them we always looked out for their welfare, that they shouldn't be afraid of us but could trust us and work with us. Usually when we came back the next time they were a little more receptive. They'd give us some food and something to drink. We never asked for anything, just waited for them to offer. It may seem a small thing but it showed them the difference between the Guard and us. They are such humble people—they almost never start a conversation. We'd look for ways to talk with them and cheer them up.

They were always surprised when they saw a woman. They'd say to me, "So young...why did you leave your mama?" They asked me if I was afraid. I explained that women were also exploited and we were working for a better life for women too. The peasant women always treated the women comrades in a special way especially when we needed something personal...They asked me about my periods, how I managed...When I told them, they'd say "poor thing." But I told them not to pity me, that it was all right...

Yaosca told us how they came out of the mountains during the last days of the war, how the columns all met in the valley and divided up to take over the towns still controlled by the Guard. That's when she was sent to Yali and saw her husband, Justo, for the last time. He was killed on July 19. Yaosca gave birth to a baby girl in the mountains. Her name is Yaosca Libertad. Justo saw the child only once, when she was fifteen days old.

YAOSCA: It was Commander Omar Cabezas who gave me the name Yaosca when I first joined the guerrilla. Yaosca, he said, was a place where the peasants gave the guerrillas a lot of support. I wanted my daughter to have that name. And Libertad? Well, my husband chose the name Libertad because she was to be born in the year of our liberation. And she was.

The Carlos Aguero Military School in Managua—the most advanced in the country—operates out of what used to be the dreaded bunker.* We talked there with several officers about the situation of women in the peacetime army. It's one thing for women to participate during a crisis period when every contribution is welcome and necessary, but it's something else again for women to take part in building the

* Somoza's "bunker," the fortified offices of the dictator on Tizcopa Hill in Managua, is now part of the *German Pomares* military complex where the *Carlos Aguero* School operates. The high command of the Sandinist People's Army is also located there.

The young military school students at the *Carlos Aguero* School, at the "German Pomares" Military Complex, in what used to be Somoza's "bunker"

army as a stable institution. Although there were numerous women in the army during the war, after the victory the training of men and women together in the same units began to raise questions. Now, in fact, they are being trained separately. We asked why.

"It's not that the women comrades aren't capable," the director of the school explained, "and it's not that we're thinking of excluding women from the army. There are women with excellent military talents, and there is room for them in our ranks. But right now we see the need for training them separately. There are exceptions of course, there are women who because of their excellence must be left in the regular army and given every opportunity to advance. The need to train women separately is not because

*of any limitations the women have. In fact, you might say
it's because of failings on the part of some men. Our army
has many new soldiers, comrades who haven't had the
experience of fighting alongside women, and they aren't
always able to relate to a woman as just another soldier.
They still tend to see them as women."*

It's clear that this is a temporary situation. Women will
be trained separately only until army discipline increases to
the point where women are viewed as "just soldiers." Even
now, however, there is a large group of comrades—male
and female—for whom this is not a problem. These are the
"Sandinitos," extremely young fighters who at the time of
the victory were thirteen, fourteen and fifteen years
old—some even younger. Today they continue their
training together, male and female.*

*We'd heard about these young soldiers. They refused to
accept scholarships and other chances to study, which the
government and the FSLN offered them at the war's end.
"We tried to separate them from military life," a
spokesperson for the army told us, "because we feel that
people so young should have a chance to study in another
context. But they wouldn't accept a discharge. They love
the Sandinist army and they know they've earned the right
to stay here. And they are right. These young people have
showed an extraordinary strength—in many cases, real
heroism. So what can we do with them? For the time being
they are studying here at the school, at the* Carlos Aguero."

*Later we met with a group of "Sandinitos." It wasn't
easy to get them to talk about their situation. Apparently all
of them see continuing in the army as the logical
consequence of their participation in the war. It doesn't
seem unusual to them. I asked Mariana, aged fifteen, how
her parents felt about her going off to fight at such a young
age. "Well," she said, "it's our responsibility to talk to our
parents and explain the situation. Children have an
obligation to make their parents more aware. I don't think
any parent who was aware of what was going on would
deny their child the chance to take part." But when we
asked her to elaborate on her experience with her parents,
she laughed and said, "I didn't tell my parents. I just left*

the house. I knew they wouldn't let me go. My papa looked for a rope to tie me up when all I was doing was taking part in student strikes! So one day I got up early, did all the chores, and left. I didn't come home until two weeks later when we retreated to Masaya."

All these young people agreed that being "Sandinitos" had greatly influenced their relationships with the opposite sex. "The developments in our country have made us mature." "Now there's more equality." "Before men gave the orders, almost always. Now women give their opinion, both women and men have opinions. . ." When asked what they would tell young people in other countries they all said, "Struggle, struggle like we did here. And parents too should struggle along with the children. Parents are the ones that sometimes tell you not to do things. It's because they are afraid. Youth everywhere has the responsibility of fighting for liberation."

Nicaragua's fighting youth have a history worthy of a book of their own. Thousands of young people gave their lives in the struggle for liberation. Many Sandinist militants were only nine, ten or eleven years old. One well-known example is Luis Alfonso Velasquez. Luis began taking part in the student movement at grade school when he was seven. He left school in the third grade to devote himself full-time to the struggle. He lost his life before his tenth birthday, murdered by a thug sent specifically to hunt him down.

There are women in Nicaragua who have taken the initiative of forming their own companies within the army. They want to circumvent any sexist tendencies within the Sandinist army and keep alive this new tradition of fighting women. We are told the first all-woman company was camped near Esteli. We went there to talk with the comrades.

It was a Sunday and we found the members of the Juana Elena Mendoza *Infantry Company on weekend leave. Some were out on passes. Others sat around the entrance to the camp talking with family or friends. We asked to speak with the leader of the group and almost immediately Rosa Adelina Barahona appeared. Her pseudonym is "Margarita." She's 20 years old, small, thin and very pleasant. After a routine check with the military command in Esteli, she invited us to come in. We also spoke with the second-in-command, Maria Elisa Navas. Maria is a lively and expressive woman, and only seventeen.*

We made ourselves comfortable in the centre patio. Other women walked around the area. Someone was replacing a wall mural with clippings of recent news. Some were cleaning their weapons while listening to rock music on a small transistor radio. Rosa Adelina and Maria Elisa became more and more enthusiastic as they told us about

Rosa

their lives—how they developed an understanding of the need to fight, how they joined the guerrilla, the transition to regular army life, and finally, their being placed in charge of this company of 130 women.

ROSA ADELINA: When I first came to the guerrilla camp you had to earn your weapon. There weren't enough to go around. At first you'd get a stick in the shape of a gun. And you couldn't lose that stick. It had to be treated with such care... That was my "gun" during training. I used to leave the stick at the edge of our hut every night. When they called us to begin our morning exercises, we'd leap out of our hammocks, put everything into our knapsacks and grab our sticks on the way out. At that time I wasn't used to any kind of exercise. I had studied at a religious school where everything was completely different.

I joined up at Quilali. My first training school was called *Juan Gregorio Colindres*. And Juan Colindres—who fought with Sandino—was my grandfather... Everyone in my family was a Sandinista. There are eight in my family and four of us became guerrillas. One died in Waslala. I also had 20 cousins in combat. My first military experience was the attack on a government service station near Ducuali. I was really afraid when the battle began. I had never even heard gunfire before. But then, when you get into it, you forget your fears. You remember you're fighting for your people...

Later, they sent me here to Esteli and I entered the military command. I was one of the first to enter. My superior officer was forming a women's squadron. I was told that I was to be the leader. On July 20 I began to work with the women.

MARIA ELISA: This company is something we thought up to show our ability and desire to belong to the army. Women want to organize militarily to defend our country. We want to show that women continue to have a role to play, that we are worth something...

Maria

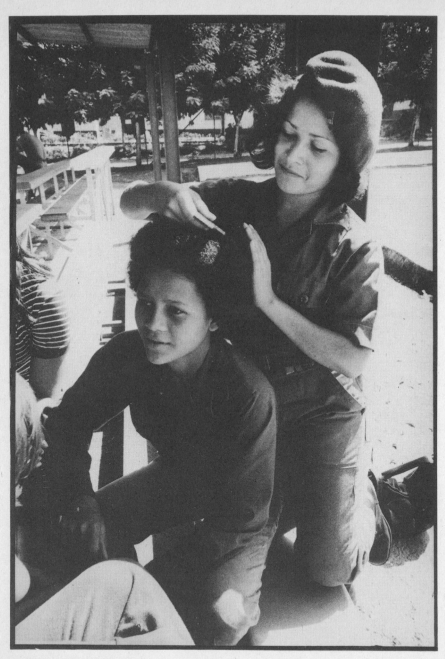

Students at the *Carlos Aguero*

ROSA ADELINA: So they won't treat us like objects, like under the old regime...

MARIA ELISA: You know, last night I went to a wedding when I was home on pass. I was talking to a fellow who asked, "But what are you doing in the army? Women are delicate..." "No!" I said, "That's not true. *I don't like it* when men think women are delicate. There's nothing I like better than a man saying 'women are equal to men.'"

We've had so many experiences, first in the guerrilla and now since liberation. Look, when Esteli was liberated—what joy we felt! We couldn't believe that Esteli was finally free. They called it Somoza's stronghold. We hugged each other. You can't imagine how happy we were. Then we left. I thought of staying in Esteli for the reconstruction but they formed a column and I had to leave. They sent us to fight at Boaco and from there we went to Managua. I didn't think I'd be back in Esteli, but two weeks later they sent us back. We finally saw Esteli with people in it. Right after we took the city, the people who had fled to the surrounding area began to return. It was so exciting. That's when I thought of the idea of a squadron of women, led by women. It was unheard of. I didn't believe it. And now, a whole company...

During our conversation a man approached us. He was the only man I'd seen there. It was Victor Perez Espinosa who, like Rosa Adelina, is a company leader. He has been the women's instructor. We talked with him about the ability of these women as fighters and briefly explored some of the prevalent ideas about women's, as opposed to men's, military ability.

VICTOR: My opinion is that men have nothing on these women. Physically women can accomplish the same. I know because I've had the experience of training both men and women. Throwing a grenade? Well, it's possible a woman might not throw it as far as a man. Often men have done more strenuous work and have developed their strength. But there are women comrades here who throw grenades 30 yards, and there are male comrades who'd have a hard time matching that. For example, in the rocket-launching contest we had a few days ago, which included men from all the different units, a woman from this unit made the best throw of all. She had the best throw in the whole region.

It's important to learn to throw a grenade or a rocket but it's also important to learn about superior war techniques which don't depend on physical strength. Most important of all is to be very clear about what we're struggling for and what we're defending. Both the women and men comrades must develop their political consciousness. They must understand that they are fighting for their people and exploited people everywhere.

When we returned to Managua and to the Carlos Aguero
*School, we had the chance to interview one of those women
the director of the school had described as an "exception."
Juana Galo is exceptional among men and women. She is
one of the school's best students and is in its most advanced
courses. A simple, modest woman, she seems to feel
completely comfortable in a military setting. When we
started talking she didn't see anything out of the ordinary
about her situation. She told her story very sparsely,
informatively but without much detail. But in the process of
recounting her experiences she became more enthusiastic
and talkative.*

JUANA: I'm nineteen years old. I was born in
Chinandega. My family is working class. My father is an
electrician, my mother a dressmaker. There are five
brothers and sisters in all. We were quite poor. My papa
earned 1,000 *cordobas* at most. It wasn't enough to run the
house so we all had to help. I took a secretarial course from
1975 to 1977 and then began to work as a secretary at the
Agricultural Institute...It was hard on my parents when I
left. They counted on the money I brought in. At the
beginning it must have been very hard, but later they
understood.

I joined the Movement of Junior High School Students in
1976. By 1977 I was working with the United People's
Movement. And in 1978 I started the process of joining the
Nicaraguan Revolutionary Youth* and was made head of
the propaganda committee in my neighbourhood. I lived in
Santa Rosa, one of the neighbourhoods in Managua that
was hardest hit by the earthquake.

From 1978 on, I gave everything I had to the Revolution.
That was the year we increased our harassment of the
National Guard. We threw bombs and distributed signs,

---

* The Nicaraguan Revolutionary Youth was the young people's branch
of the Proletarian tendency of the FSLN. After the three tendencies
united it remained as the youth group of the FSLN. Since the victory it
has changed its name to the *July 19* Sandinist Youth Movement.

Juano Galo

pamphlets and FSLN flags. We used to stay on the streets
until one or two in the morning pasting up handbills. We
worked hard to raise the consciousness of people in the
neighbourhoods, our friends, and the people we worked
with. We were preparing for battle, organizing neighbourhood civil defence committees, etc. Everyone helped make
trenches and barricades. Then in 1979 I took part in the
attack on the Agricultural Institute where I worked. It was
great; we took my boss, the director, prisoner.

I became a commander after my group leader Combo was
killed. He was one of the first comrades to die. I was leader
of three zones. It was a big job. There were two clinics in the
zones, which made my tasks even more difficult. It got so
that I couldn't keep track of the days. I would get up at one
o'clock in the morning—that's if I even had a chance to go
to sleep—to prepare the medicines at one of the clinics. Then
I would make the rounds of all the wounded. I also had to
find time to inspect the trenches in all three zones. I almost
never had time to eat. Often I'd just have water to keep me
going. That's the way things went until we withdrew.

There were 125 women in the column I was in. All of us—men and women—were very close. We thought of each other as brothers and sisters. I remember there were twelve of us who pretty well lived together. There were no mattresses or beds; we'd just sleep where we could, sharing a couple of jackets to cover ourselves. If one of us got hold of a piece of candy, we all shared it. We even co-operated when we took baths. A bath consisted of throwing water on yourself—no soap, towel, nothing. One of the comrades would stand watch outside while another washed up. It was a family. If something happened to one of us we all felt it.

I got injured once. We were on a mission to rout out some of the Guard. They shelled us that night. They didn't usually use bombs at night but by that time they were trying anything. During the shelling I caught a piece of shrapnel in one lung. They took me to a hospital but I wouldn't stay. I would have gone back even if it had been serious, even if the doctor had ordered me to stay. I knew they needed every last one of us on the line.

I was a barracks leader in Jinotepe when the victory came. Then I came here. Last August I began a class for squadron leader and then for platoon leader. Right now I'm taking the company and battalion leaders' course. Each is six months long.

I love army life. Being here I can do everything possible for reconstruction and for our people. We owe everything we are to our people. As long as I live, I want to serve them.

Girl, simple girl
with your own liberation begun
Allow my verses of love
to entwine themselves in your gun.

The people who know the dawn of freedom
is coming soon, somehow
recognize your heroic struggles
girl, you're a woman now.*

* Last verse of the song "Girl of the Sandinist Front."

Seven

Sister Martha—
Women of Hope

The city of Matagalpa nestles in a deep valley in north-western Nicaragua. Its narrow streets and market-plaza are alive with the comings and goings of the cattle and coffee industries on which it depends. To one side, on the surrounding hills, lies the cemetery. And across the way there's the spot "where the M-50 stood, the cannon they used to shoot us down."

The Santa Teresita School is also located atop one of the surrounding hills, not far from the city. It was from this school that the sisters actively supported the people in the struggle against the dictatorship. We arrived at the simple cement building on a November morning. We were looking for Sister Martha, the school's most public and well-known representative. Sister Martha is a symbol of that part of the Catholic Church in Nicaragua which has consistently fought to bring the church's daily practice in line with its preaching.

We wanted to speak to Sister Martha about the movement taking place in the Latin American church, a church which throughout its history had invariably allied itself with the ruling classes. Now, however, there are signs of a new life, a life more in agreement with its teachings. This change began with isolated cases: a small group of Maryknolls in Guatemala, a nun tortured by the repressive *forces in Brazil, the "Priests for Socialism" movement in Chile... And there are the well-known examples of individuals like Ernesto Cardenal in Nicaragua and Camilo Torres in Colombia who have made it clear that the worker-priest tradition—long-known in Europe—is developing in Latin America. But all too often, and in spite of people like Silva Henriquez, Obando y Bravo* and other prelates who have become mediators between the present-day dictatorships and the people they repress, the church's position—as a whole—still supports reaction over the people.*

The progressive movement within the church will not be stopped. As I write these pages, news comes of the murder of Archbishop Oscar Arnulfo Romero in El Salvador, confirming once more that within as well as outside the church there are men and women who proclaim—with their lives—that nothing can defeat the people rising up in the just struggle for their rights. Archbishop Romero had repeatedly and publicly asserted the right of the Salvadoreans to take up arms. He saw no contradiction between his religious beliefs and socialism. Because of this, government reactionaries had him gunned down as he led a mass in El Salvador's main cathedral. He becomes one more in a long list of martyrs in this continental people's war.

But let's get back to Sister Martha. As we stepped from our jeep Sister Martha came out of the school to greet us. A serene, unadorned and open face smiled at us from the white habit. She reminded me of the nuns of my childhood: those mysterious beings I'd see on the streets—always in pairs—who, because of their distance from my world, I never quite knew how to place. She invites us into a simple room and we begin to talk.

---

* Archbishop Silva Henriquez of Santiago de Chile is active in the struggle against the fascist Junta in that country. Archbishop Obando y Bravo of Managua assumed a position in support of the revolutionary movement against the Somoza dictatorship long before the victory. He often acted as mediator in actions like the occupation of the National Palace in August 1978. Unfortunately, since the victory in Nicaragua he has moved further to the right and now represents the right-wing in the church.

Sister Martha

SISTER MARTHA: My name is Martha Deyanira Frech
Lopez, but everyone calls me Sister Martha. I was born
here in Matagalpa in 1943, the same year as Doris Maria
Tijerino.* Doris and I were childhood friends. We went to
the San Jose School together. I'll always remember her as a
very intelligent child, very analytical. Even when she was
very young she always seemed to know what she wanted to
do, that she wanted to fight against injustice. Those of us
who are Doris' and my age have never really known
anything except oppression. She was always incensed by the
lack of justice in our country. Doris was one of those who
sparked our love for Nicaragua and for the oppressed.

I always wanted to follow her example, as did others in
our class at San Jose. Monsenior Calderon y Padilla
always said he was worried about what might happen to
Doris because she was so young. He said her cause was just,
and it was commendable that we wanted to follow her
example, but we were too young and it was too dangerous
for us just to go off like Doris, to go underground, with all
those men. He wanted us to study to be nuns and assured us
we could do work with the peasants and the poor and raise
their consciousness through religious work.

It's people like Monsenior Calderon y Padilla who have
pushed whole sections of the church to come out in favour
of social change. He was one of the first priests to adopt an
aggressive attitude in defense of the exploited. He was very
supportive of trade union militants and often took part in
public events. He didn't care if they were communists. And
he was always at the student demonstrations; he'd walk
right in front so the Guard wasn't able to be as brutal as it
might otherwise have been.

I remember once when Doris was still above ground—I
think we must have been in sixth grade—we went into the
streets protesting the student massacre of July 23.† We were

---

* Doris Maria Tijerino, a well-known militant and leader in the FSLN.
See *Doris Tijerino: Inside the Nicaraguan Revolution* (New Star Books,
1978) for an account of her life.
† On July 23, 1959 Somoza's repressive forces shot into a peaceful
student demonstration in Leon. Four were killed and over a hundred
wounded.

marching along Main Street down near the San Jose School when all of a sudden three BECATS* appeared on the scene and threw tear gas bombs at us. They were going to arrest us but Monsenior arrived and asked the police to let us go and he'd be responsible for us. He saved us from the police, but contrary to what they might have thought, he had no intention of getting us to stop our march. He joined us and continued the demonstration. His support helped a lot because he was part of the church hierarchy. He died some time ago. Monsenior was an important influence on a lot of us.

When I was still quite young I made the decision to combine a religious and political vocation. I remember the Bishop of Matagalpa always said that as a nun I could also fight like Doris Maria: she on the battlefield and me from the convent. I never saw any contradiction between socialism and Christianity. Christ came to preach a liberating religion not an opium for the people. He was a man steeped in the problems of his people. He didn't agree with the corrupt government of his day. So for me, the way to be sure of not betraying the gospel is by standing beside my people. The problem is that many sections of the church have betrayed the gospel's message. They've preached an alienating faith that works against the people's interests.

Another woman enters the room and accepts Sister Martha's invitation to sit and talk with us. She is Pilar Ximeno, the Mother Superior of this congregation of Missionaries of Charity. She is older than Sister Martha but has the same vitality. In spite of her many years in Nicaragua, she retains her Spanish accent. The three of us talked about their involvement in events in Matagalpa.

SISTER MARTHA: Matagalpa has a long and beautiful history of struggle. I'd say it was the students who first had the courage to fight. The student movement developed in

* BECATS were police vehicles.

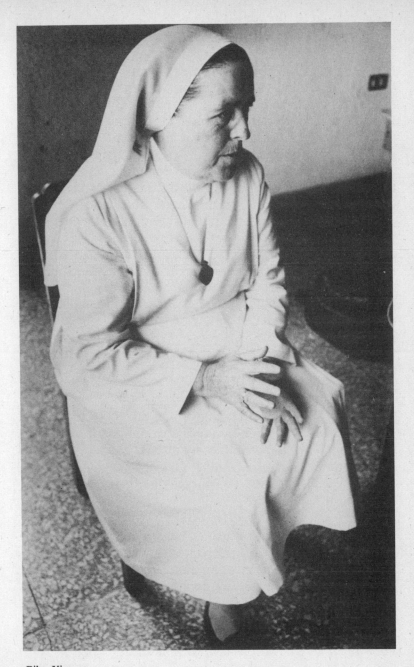

Pilar Ximeno

about 1959. It was well underway when Doris Maria and I studied at San Jose. But it got a lot stronger around 1977. Our vanguard, the FSLN, was more organized by that time and was providing good leadership. There was increasing repression and tragic losses of young lives, but there was also a series of actions that inspired faith in the students and in the people as a whole. As the movement got stronger more and more people were able to commit themselves.

By 1978, with the death of Pedro Joaquin Chamorro and the big general strike, the people lost their fear of repression and of the National Guard. There were many groups involved in analyzing the national situation and working to politicize different sections of the population. It was a time of intense political activity. Militants from the student movement visited the slum neighbourhoods and began doing political work. That was a determining factor for many of these students. When you come into contact with real misery you have no choice but to become a revolutionary.

By that time the take overs in the schools were becoming an everyday occurrence.

MOTHER PILAR: The take overs began in Matagalpa in 1976. As they became more and more political I could see that something important was taking shape, that the Revolution itself was coming. This increase in political activity wasn't isolated to Matagalpa. It was happening throughout the country.

SISTER MARTHA: We sisters helped in every way we could. In the September insurrection—which actually began in August here—we acted as mediators between the students and the Guard. We could see a massacre in the making and wanted to prevent it. We were working at the Red Cross office and saw all the war materials streaming in from Managua. We were in contact with the young people and knew they were in no position to take on the Guard. They had very few weapons and what they did have was of poor quality. To prevent a slaughter we formed a mediating commission—Monsenior y Bravo, Doctor Amador Kul,* Mother Pilar and myself—and managed to negotiate a truce with the National Guard commander:

The Guard never really honoured that truce. Naively, we went from command to command telling our fighters that the Guard had signed a truce. We told them to retreat because they didn't have a chance. But instead of a truce the Guard took the opportunity to assassinate the family of one of the student militants. We continued our support work, reported on the weaponry that was coming into the city and helped with the tactical retreat. We also helped those militants who had to get to Managua. We found people in the Christian community who could get them to Managua or hide them in their homes. We found safehouses for 150 comrades. Many progressive Christians helped the comrades.

As a result of our involvement the National Guard began to persecute us, especially me. They knew we identified with the young people and claimed we were holding "communist marxist" meetings here at the school. They threatened me. The rumour spread that the guards were saying that the "little nun is gonna have an accident." I wasn't afraid but it was decided that I should go away for awhile. I agreed to go if I was ordered but it wasn't what I wanted. If we're willing to struggle alongside the young people we must also assume the consequences, right?

Before arrangements could be made for me to leave we got involved in another incident. Some comrades from Esteli—where the repression was very bad—came to beg us to set up a mediating commission to stop the Guard from its murderous attacks. When we got to Esteli, the *compas*† said it was urgent that we get Father Julio Lopez out of the city. The Guard was looking for him and was going to kill him. There was a reward of 10,000 *cordobas* on his head. Father Julio was at Our Lady of the Rosary School where they were taking care of some refugees. When we finally reached

* Kul was the president of the Nicaraguan Red Cross.
† *Compa* is the Nicaraguan version of comrade, *companero*, etc.

him we were able to convince him to leave, after much persuasion. We dressed him in a Red Cross smock and managed to get him back here to school. We hid him for about a week before we were able to arrange his escape through one of the embassies. Mother Pilar had asked the Papal Nuncio we used to have to hide him at the nunciature. We knew he'd be safer there. The Papal Nuncio refused. That made it clear to us that there were people in the church who didn't support our struggle.

The plan was for me to leave the country at the same time as Father Julio. The Revolution had its own intelligence and they discovered that both Father Julio and I were on Immigration's blacklist. That meant we couldn't get out of Matagalpa legally. We had to find some other way to get out. I put on a pair of blue jeans and a wig. Dr. Rizo was in charge of making me up and my sister Olga styled a "hip" hairdo for Father Julio. We managed to get out of Matagalpa without any trouble. Although we were stopped at every guardpost, often by guards that knew me, no one recognized us. We hid in Managua for awhile and then sought asylum. Father Julio went to the Colombian Embassy and I to the Costa Rican.

I left Nicaragua on September 27, 1978. Somoza's people said I was being paid by "the international communist movement." Imagine—I don't even know what the international communist movement might be, I really don't. When a guard told Mother Pilar that I was being paid by the international communist movement, my response was, "If the church is communist because it struggles for justice, well I guess that makes me a communist."

I hated being away. I never could get used to watching the bullfight from the stands, I wanted to be with my people through their struggle. In Costa Rica we did public relations work. We wanted to explain what was really happening in Nicaragua; we gave interviews and held press conferences. We even spoke on the BBC of London and explained that what was happening in our country was a people's insurrection. After Costa Rica I went to Honduras where I made contact with the FSLN representative. We organized a group called Progressive Christian Youth and began to do solidarity work. We raised money, gathered blood donations for the war, etc. We did everything we could from where we were.

While I was in Honduras I met and worked with Commander Henry Ruiz.* He made a great impression on me. He's a very modest man, very intelligent and a true revolutionary. He asked me if I would be willing to carry out a mission that would involve leaving Honduras. I didn't hesitate in making a decision. I left that day for Panama and from there I went on to Costa Rica. I was ready to do any work that was needed to support the struggle in Nicaragua.

When the war ended I returned to Nicaragua—here to the school. There was and is an enormous amount of work to be done. We have work for years to come. We've been carrying on political Christian seminars at the school to raise consciousness among the young people. We want to make sure people know that the Revolution isn't completed yet, that we have to keep building it day by day. There are still many sacrifices to be made.

Progressives in the church have a continuing responsibility to see that it supports the Revolution. There are certain sections and groups in the church who are trying to set Nicaraguans against the revolutionary process. If we who are leaders in the Christian community are afraid of the revolutionary process we're going to have a negative influence on all the students and people we teach. The current Papal Nuncio was very clear about this at a national meeting held recently in Managua. "The Christian," he said, "must be a person of hope. We can't be afraid of ghosts." Progressives know we must become part of the revolutionary process. The Revolution doesn't forbid Christians living their faith, but it must be a faith in line with the interests of the great majority of our people. We must unite to work together.

Church people—priests and nuns—showed we were with

* Henry Ruiz, Commander of the Revolution, is a member of the FSLN National Leadership and Minister of Planning in the new government.

This sign represents the efforts of the most reactionary wing of the Catholic Church to get believers to reject the revolution. It reads: "We are Catholics. We love the Virgin. Do Not Bother Us."

the people during the war. There are many examples. The Maryknoll nuns at Open 3 were arrested and beaten by the Guard. In August, when we worked on a mediating commission here, the National Guard was shooting at us from the bank and we practically had to crawl along the ground to get out. The church has showed that it can identify with the people. This is the kind of church the Revolution needs in Nicaragua right now. Not a conformist church. We must help our people build our country. We must become part of history, not go against it.

This wasn't to be the last conversation we had with Sister Martha. The next time we were in Matagalpa we took the opportunity to visit the school and observed Sister Martha

Sister Martha

putting into practice her belief that the church must be part of the revolutionary process. While we were there we saw truck loads of women driving up. They were from Christian communities in various neighbourhoods. They had come for a showing of the German film September 1978, *an impressive record of the Nicaraguan people's insurrection.*

SISTER MARTHA: Nicaraguan society is very sexist. Women have always been considered objects of sexual satisfaction. They are supposed to be submissive to their husband and to obligingly take care of the household duties and the children. Nicaraguan women want to change their situation. They have taken an active part in the Revolution not only to achieve freedom for the people but also to achieve their own freedom as women. It's my view that in a place like Nicaragua the Revolution means women's liberation as well.

What do you think of this slogan, *Women of Hope—Consolidate Our Revolution*? I've written a few words to read to the women who have come to see the film today.

Today Nicaraguan women hold Mary the Mother of God as their first model for promoting this Revolution. She too carried to the world a message of liberation... Mary isn't the sugar-sweet stupid woman reactionary Christians so often make her out to be. At the age of fifteen—the same age as Doris Maria Tijerino—she took an active part in the liberation of her people. She doesn't speak of individual moralistic changes, but of the reorganization of the social order into one which there are no rich and poor, powerful and humble. And so, faced with this new dawn filled with great hopes and with Christian and revolutionary responsibilities, Nicaraguan women must follow the path begun by Mary of Nazareth and Doris Maria of Matagalpa. We have but one alternative: *To be women of hope working for the consolidation of our revolution.*

Eight
Gladys Baez

...we die as often as we
let our eyelids close on memory
—RICARDO MORALES, PANCASAN

In Pancasan, during those days in 1967 when our leaders went off to do their planning, we—the rank and file—dreamed about the future. We decided that even if only one of us survived, he or she would remain in the countryside and build city-farms. We traced the outline of a city-farm on the ground and joked and argued about what it would be like. Everyone had their say. That's why this commune bears the name *Rigoberto Cruz-Pablo Ubeda*—in memory of the heroes of Pancasan.

Along the Leon-Poneloya road there's an agricultural commune that will one day be a thriving city-farm. Gladys Baez, a dedicated long-time member of the Sandinist National Liberation Front heads Rigoberto Cruz-Pablo Ubeda. *When we arrived looking for Gladys, we met a group of children playing on an old grinding machine in the stable by the commune entrance. They pointed to an ancient wooden staircase which took us to a loft where two young men were working over a huge accounting book. Gladys had been called to Leon and hadn't been able to wait for us. One of the men offered to show us the way so we climbed back in our jeep and set out for Leon. Before we reached the city we lost sight of our lead car, but as we slowly made our way through the streets of Leon's outlying neighbourhoods, we spotted the old red car. Our comrade waved to us from the doorway of one of the houses. We were invited inside and introduced to Gladys Baez, known in this area as Luisa.*

Gladys' peasant background is apparent in her appearance. She is short, with a stocky body and almost Indian facial features. She wears pants and work boots. Two thick braids fall to mid-chest. Her eyes reveal a combination of determination and innocence. Against her dark rayon blouse hangs an image of Che carved on a wooden star.

Without wasting any time—there's always work to be done—we pull together a couple of wooden chairs in the back patio and begin to tape. To begin with, Gladys can't remember the year she was born. She says she's very forgetful, but that a few days ago she was 38 and laughingly challenges us to "figure it out for yourselves." Surrounded by children and chickens, in a yard that soon feels like home, we first talk about the importance of her telling us about her life. She felt uncomfortable, repeating several times some variation on "no one really likes to talk about themselves." But this sparkling and energetic woman is a real storyteller and in no time she began sharing the details of her life.

GLADYS: I was born in Juigalpa, in the district of Chontales. I never really knew my father; it was my mother who raised me. I owe much of what I am today to her. I was her only child and she was 42 when I was born. She worked incredibly hard, washing and ironing to support the two of us. And she was a humanitarian, always helping other people with their problems. She became a grandmother to the entire neighbourhood; everyone called her grandma.

There was nothing very unusual about my childhood. My mother wanted the best for me so she kept me close to the church. By the time I was seven I was the prayer girl for the neighbourhood. I knew just about every prayer there was. I

was also in other religious groups. But in spite of all that church stuff, I never really allowed myself to become totally convinced by religion. I went to church to make my mother happy, but deep down I was a lively kid and full of fun. It wasn't long before I could see through the whole alms game and was ready for a change.

By the time I was twelve or so I had left the piety of the church and thrown myself into the social scene. Dances and parties became my life and for the next few years there was no stopping me. If I couldn't find a party I invented one.

I'd celebrate my birthday three times a year just to get a good party going. But during this period I also started getting involved in the Workers Club. One thing I'll say for myself, that society stuff never went to my head. I always knew my class.

In 1956 I married a man who was involved in the workers movement. He was a member of the Socialist Party. I was still pretty empty-headed and had a lot of crazy ideas, but after I got married I was often around political discussions, and slowly began participating in political work.

I got much more involved after the killing of Somoza Garcia.* The authorities rounded up everyone they thought might be connected with the opposition. Many people went to jail, and my husband was one of them. I was pregnant by then but, big belly and all, I started working for his release. I joined with the other mothers and wives and went to the prison. We brought the men food and monitored how they were being treated. We worked together and did things like visit the commander's wife. At that point we weren't even demanding freedom for our prisoners—just that they receive humane treatment. A lot of women took part. Wherever you have prisoners you generally have the mothers, wives and daughters turning out every day. Men may give money for support but women lend a physical presence.

There were people in my neighbourhood and social circle who read and studied books that were much more political than any I'd ever seen. Even though I'd only gone to the third grade, I loved to read. But the books I read were mostly cheap romantic novels. Once a friend of mine brought me a copy of Gorki's *Mother*. It was completely different from anything I was used to so at first I didn't pay much attention to it. I let a month go by and returned the book. I hadn't even read it, but when I talked to Miguel I said I found it very interesting. I'm sure he knew I hadn't opened it and that my comment was only a courtesy— though he knew manners had never been my strong point.

* On September 21, 1956 Rigoberto Lopez Perez executed the dictator Somoza Garcia. Rigoberto was killed the same day by Somoza's bodyguards.

He began explaining parts of the book to me and I got so interested that I borrowed it back and read it from beginning to end. It made quite an impact on me.

My next involvement, after working with the prisoners, was to join the workers and peasants union in our area. That was in 1958. Through the union we organized classes in the countryside and town to teach people practical skills. We covered the whole district of Chontales. Chontales is a very backward area, both politically and economically. Even today they still use ploughs pulled by oxen. And that economic backwardness influences the level of political maturity. Organizing in this area was always very difficult. That was why part of our work was to teach real skills to the people. One of our projects in my town was to set up a free night school for children. Back then there were no night schools, even though many kids couldn't go to school in the day. Most mothers had to spend all day down at the river washing clothes and needed their children with them. Our school was a big hit but the authorities got tough with us almost immediately.

There were rumours that it was a communist school and that we weren't teaching the children to believe in God. The town priest used the entire Holy Week to denounce us. He attacked the school in all his talks and sermons. At first he just criticized the school, without mentioning any names. But soon he began making references to "the school mistress." The only "mistress" was me; the others were all men. My mother was quite upset when he pointed the finger at me. She took me aside and said, "Look, this is going to be bad for you. I know you've got your reasons for being involved, but why don't you go and talk to the priest and get him to stop bothering you?" I took her advice and went to pay the man a visit. Fifteen of my students went with me.

I knew that if the children's parents got wind of what the priest was saying they would withdraw their children from our school. So when I met with the priest I challenged him to start his own school if ours bothered him so much. And that's what happened. The next year there was another free school for students from first through sixth grades. It all turned out quite well.

I continued to get more involved. At a May Day meeting in 1960, I gave my first public speech. We did a lot of work organizing that year's event. We had a parade and staged a meeting. I was one of four speakers talking about the significance of May 1. Since I'd never spoken in public before, I was given the theme in advance so I'd have time to prepare. Once I had the talk prepared, I consulted some of the other comrades, who assured me it was O.K. Anyway, I wasn't too worried about making a mistake. I always figured that if I did, someone would correct me and that would be that.

I remember a time when I did make a mistake. It was at one of our first union meetings. A few of the key members were late in arriving so we started the meeting without them. By the time they arrived we had made a number of very important decisions. I was supposed to report these decisions and started off by saying, "Well, comrades, this was a great meeting. We did all we had to. We changed our executive in a *diplomatic* way." I was then informed that the word was *democratic* not *diplomatic*. "No problem," I said. I never was one for shutting up. I always went right ahead and made my mistakes so they could teach me how it was supposed to be done. That's how I learned.

But I was telling you about that May 1 meeting and my experience as a public speaker. My speech was well-received. Representatives from the Socialist Party were at the meeting and one of them, a comrade named Chaguitillo, suggested I represent the party at the Moscow Women's Congress that year. They had other candidates in mind, strong, active women from different parts of the country, each of whom could do a good job representing Nicaraguan women. But since I was a working class woman he proposed that they send me. He must have been convincing because a short while later they asked me to go.

Imagine! I'd never even been to Managua and here I was being asked to attend a conference in the Soviet Union. When they came to talk to me about it I told them my husband would probably not like the idea. I knew he would want me to stay home with the kids. "If you tell him you're sending me to the Soviet Union you can forget it," I said.

"You won't get me out of Juigalpa even if you tie me up and drag me out. So let's put our heads together and come up with a plan." I suggested that they tell people in the party that I was going to Costa Rica to take a course and that I'd be coming back to work at the school again. We arranged with my mother to stay with my little girl and told my husband he had to stay in Nicaragua. People suspected something funny was going on, but they thought I was going off to Cuba. The Cuban Revolution was in full swing by then. When I left some people said, "When you see Fidel, give him a kiss for me."

I went to Managua for eight days before leaving for the Soviet Union. My time in Managua was spent preparing for the conference. The party wanted me to be prepared, to absorb everything I would need to know in order to participate. There was a lot to learn but that didn't really worry me. I told them, "I'll learn what I can, and that will have to do."

We worked under tremendous limitations then and that made getting to Moscow very complicated. From Managua I had to get in touch with a comrade in Mexico who was to make the final arrangements for me to get to Moscow. The conference was going strong by the time I arrived and I just plunged in. There were many issues that I couldn't really talk about. It was 1962 and the differences between Russia and China were just emerging. The Chinese delegates were putting forward their thesis, the Russians theirs. I didn't say anything at all. "Let them fight over it," I thought, "and may the best side win!"

I was very anxious to give a report on Nicaragua that would have an impact on people. I worked with the interpreter before I gave the report so that it would be translated properly into the various languages. The work paid off. While I gave my report many of the delegates were busy making notes. Something must have been getting through.

The Congress was a wonderful and important experience for me. I really learned a lot, more than I would have from 100 books. I went with a lot of crazy ideas and prejudices, but by the time I returned I had matured a lot. Once back in

Nicaragua I joined the Socialist Party. I began to work toward establishing a women's organization in Nicaragua. That's when we started the Organization of Democratic Women. I worked with women and at the same time continued my work in the union.

The years 1963 and 1964 were terrible, especially here in the mountains. The repression was brutal. They were burning farms and jailing people. In 1965 we staged a huge demonstration in Managua that involved hundreds of peasants from Matagalpa, Jinotega, Esteli, Rivas and Chontales. We went on foot. It was quite an experience.

We brought the best and most conscious people to that demonstration. Who would walk so many miles if they weren't already politically conscious? The most militant peasant and worker organizations were there. When we got to Managua we walked right into the Workers House without permission. Some people told us we would have to leave but we weren't having any of that. "This is a workers house," we said, "and we're workers." We ended up staying for eight days.

It was a busy time. There were meetings every day. Students came around to talk to us. We went to the Chamber of Deputies to meet with the officers. We also carried out a hunger strike. Within eight days the leaders were thrown in jail and the authorities tried to ship the rest back where we had come from.

Six of us were arrested. We were on a hunger strike at the time so we just continued it in jail. For the most part we were in good spirits and were sure of our principles. After six days in jail, they brought us before a police court and the judge sentenced us to 180 days, without the right of appeal. We decided to continue our strike.

By this time newspaper reporters were desperate to get in. Right from the beginning they had come to the prison and insisted on seeing us and finding out how we were. I had an interesting experience with them. Under the old regime when prisoners knew the press was around they would shout out their names so they would know who was there. That's what I did but somehow things got mixed up. The next day there was an article in *La Prensa* which said the authorities had me naked and hanging from my toes. My jailers were very upset by that article. They kept begging me to respond, to say the article was a lie. It's true they hadn't treated us badly. They'd even brought us good restaurant food to encourage us to eat. But I didn't want to make any statements, knowing they could later be used against me. They hadn't touched us that time, but what about the next?

Students and peasants were active in working for our release. The authorities thought they could solve the problem by putting the peasants on trucks and sending them home. Many returned and refused to leave while we were in prison. That, combined with the article, had an effect on the authorities. The government didn't want a scandal. They weren't taking the same dictatorial and brutal positions they assumed later. They wanted to show a certain level of stability, so they were playing the good guys.

After my stay in jail something happened which made it easy for me to make the transition from the Socialist Party to the FSLN. When I left the prison I went straight to the party house. While I was there I got into a conversation with a comrade. First he told me how the party had had faith in my ability to stand up to whatever I might face in prison. They knew I'd hold up O.K. Then he went on to say that people had been making some unfavourable comments about a conversation I'd had one evening at the Workers House before we got arrested. The whole thing was nothing more than pure prejudice. I was a married woman and had been seen talking to a man late at night.

I was furious. While I was in jail going hungry my "comrades" on the outside were gossiping about me being a whore. That's just the way I put it to him and it had an impact. He arranged for me to see the general secretary to discuss the matter. But when I met the general secretary, instead of discussing the problem, he offered me money to send to my kids. They knew I had no money and was working as a volunteer, but just the same, it felt like a slap in the face. As soon as he gave me the money I tore it up right there in front of him. "If I wanted to go begging," I said, "I'd go down to the market. I could make a lot more money there." When it comes to my principles, I don't care who I'm talking to, even the highest leader; I say what I believe. And that's when I left the party.

That wasn't the first time I'd had problems with the party. There was an incident shortly after I returned from the Congress in the Soviet Union. When I got home the local priest excommunicated me. I don't know if you can understand what that means in a small town. It affects your relations with almost everyone. I had a little store, and after I was excommunicated no one would buy from me. I made my living making clothes but no one would buy what I made. I couldn't support myself. The party's response was to suggest I move to Managua and earn a living by working for the party. But I couldn't just leave with that kind of situation in my home town. I had to try to break down that barrier.

I lived half a block from the local hospital and since no one was speaking to me I began to visit the health centre. Sick people rarely hear about excommunications and besides, there are many sick people whom nobody visits. I went and talked with them. I got hold of a camera and tape recorder and began gathering testimony about the disastrous conditions in the centre. I took pictures, taped people's testimonies and did whatever other kinds of investigation I could.

Once the investigation was completed I began organizing a campaign against the situation in that hospital. One of the doctors got involved. His sister died as a result of deficiencies in the hospital system, and her death prompted him to join the campaign. We planned a meeting at which I showed my pictures and played my tapes. We also started a petition, demanding that the director of the hospital be replaced and that conditions be improved. We were able to involve lots of people in the campaign.

As a result of that meeting the Juigalpa police fined me 10,000 *cordobas*; of course I couldn't pay it, so I set out to raise the money. I was seven months pregnant at the time and took full advantage of that. People tend to be a bit afraid of pregnant women and they certainly don't want them going to prison. When I went from house to house trying to raise the money, people were very sympathetic.

It was out of this work that I was able to break down the anger and suspicions about me that the priest had set up.

People in the town could see that despite the blows I received I wasn't going to let the authorities defeat me. In the end we were able to force the authorities to remove the director of the hospital and the chief of police.

Ultimately, this chain of events also affected my marriage. The problem was sexism. My husband never really wanted me to get involved in anything beyond union work, and that political difference between us caused problems in our relationship. He kept pressuring me to stay home where I could be a proper wife and mother. My excommunication from the church, regular political involvement, and initiative around the hospital campaign made our situation worse. Finally everything was just too much for my husband and we separated.

After I left the Socialist Party I wanted to continue being part of an organization. The FSLN was out to recruit me but at the time I was critical of it. What I knew about the FSLN came mostly from the Socialist Party. I was convinced that it was a group of opportunists and adventurers, so I wasn't very open to them at first.

They sent Efrain Sanchez to talk to me. He explained the difference between the political lines of the two organizations, primarily in terms of the FSLN's position on the need for armed struggle vis-a-vis the Socialist Party's commitment to a peaceful transition. I was already skeptical about the party's pacifist line. They believed they were going to achieve benefits for the working class little by little. That didn't seem workable to me. But I still had many doubts about the FSLN and wasn't willing to listen to them. Efrain went back to the Organization and said there was no use talking to me.

Some time later they sent Danilo Rosales around. He would visit me every afternoon at four o'clock. We became great friends—most of the time our conversation didn't touch on politics. Then, little by little, he began to raise political topics: what the Socialist Party is, what the FSLN is, and the differences between them. And many others. To make a long story short, I told him to give me eight days to think things over. Then I joined the FSLN.

That's the story of how I left the party, smoothed things

over in my home town, separated from my husband, and became a member of the FSLN.

My first task after joining the FSLN was working in safehouses in Managua. The leadership soon came to the conclusion that I should be in the mountains. Because of my previous experience working with peasants in Matagalpa and Jinotega they thought I should be in the rural guerrilla. So into the mountains I went. By that time there were a number of women taking part in the cities. Martha Narvaez, Doris Tijerino and Michele Najlis were working in the Organization. Women worked in safehouses and in the student movement, but there still weren't any women in the mountains. Doris used to come and go bringing supplies, but I was the first woman who went to stay and work in the mountains. Later there were more women in the camps. From 1967 to the present, women have participated in all aspects of the Organization's work.

Efrain and I went to the mountains together, pretending to be a married couple. That made the Guard less suspicious. Other comrades were waiting for us just outside Matagalpa. We connected with them and then we all had to walk for three days to reach the camp. When we arrived the reception we received was incredible. The solidarity really moved me. We'd taken so long they had thought we were dead, so when we finally did arrive there was a big celebration. Later we were formally initiated into the guerrilla ranks.

My particular responsibility was visiting the villages and trying to gain the confidence and support of the peasants. Others had already begun this work and over time we were able to build up a solid support among the peasants. They would keep our presence secret and warn us when it was too dangerous for us to come near the village.

In addition to our specific work, each of us participated in the general life of the detachment—the hikes, exercises and studies. We all studied political theory, practiced guerrilla tactics and simulated combat situations. I wasn't used to the strenuous exercises and the weight we had to carry, but I managed. I stayed at the camp for several months, until I had to return to the city for an operation. I didn't want to go back to the city even with the problems in my health. Here's what happened.

At the end of July, two peasants defected from our ranks and the whole column was called together. Carlos Reyna spoke about the FSLN's program and statutes. He reminded us that the statutes stipulated the death penalty for traitors. He said if any of us wanted to leave, and went immediately, the Organization wouldn't apply the death penalty. If any of us felt we couldn't take it, he said, we should quit now. He gave us half an hour to think it over.

There were some who expected me to leave. Many of the comrades still weren't used to a woman in the column. At times they would joke around and ask why I hadn't stayed in the city. Or they would tell me I was slowing the guerrilla down. When Carlos gave us the ultimatum, some of the comrades looked at me as if to say "go on, leave." But I reminded myself that I'd come to stay and they had no right to intimidate me.

No one made a move. Everyone just waited out the half-hour, and once it had passed, Carlos started crying. It was the first and only time I ever saw him cry. Then the kidding started. We punched and hugged each other. And everyone laughed. We acted like a bunch of kids. Carlos and Silvio spoke at once, saying they knew all along that neither I nor anyone else would leave.

Shortly after that incident I left for the city. It was because I left then that I didn't die at Pancasan. It was my squadron that perished there. It was terribly hard for me to accept the news of my comrades' deaths. I couldn't believe it. I was part of all the preparations and had worked closely with everyone in the squadron. Their deaths were a real blow.

I was arrested again in 1967. I was working and recuperating in a safehouse in Managua. The doctors had decided on a long medical treatment instead of an operation; I had a problem with my ovaries and seven different parasites. Of course a jail is no place to get well. I was sentenced to two months in solitary, during which time they subjected me to all kinds of tortures. They weren't using the hood then so you could see everything they did to you and who was doing it. The electric shocks were the worst.

They treated me so badly the military doctors gave me up for lost. They didn't think I'd make it. When I got out the revolutionary doctors said the same thing. No one could agree on the extent of my injuries. But I refused to accept the fact that I was going to die, although I didn't think I would recover as much as I have. It took me two years.

I decided to go to stay with my mother because I knew I would be a drain on the Organization and my friends. Silently I returned to my family. My children were grown by this time and I thought I could devote my last days to them. But it was difficult at home. My mother hadn't known about my political activities so the last thing she expected was for me to return home suffering from the effects of torture. She found my being home very difficult. Finally I decided to go and live with an aunt.

On top of my difficult living situation, my health was still very bad. I suffered from fits and often couldn't control myself. I was like that for a long time. Then slowly I began to improve. After a while I could leave the farmhouse occasionally to go into Juigalpa. I felt a tremendous need to work and participate, but I couldn't do much at first. Every time I tried to do something it turned out wrong. My head always ached. And I'd forget things. Little by little I was able to rehabilitate myself. It took a long time but I did get better. I stopped feeling like an old rag no one cared about or remembered. I looked for ways to co-operate in the revolutionary process and tried to avoid letting myself get depressed over what I couldn't do.

It was awful not to be able to be as involved as I had been. I used to dream up different projects to keep busy. During the strike by mothers of political prisoners, I embroidered ten pillow cases with the image of Sandino on them, one for each of the mothers. I didn't have money to buy good material and the cheap material I did buy kept getting caught in my machine. I ended up having to sew them by hand. While the mothers went hungry I sewed.

I finished the last pillow case the day the strike ended. You think up some crazy projects when you need to be contributing. Of course there's nothing very necessary about making pillow cases, but it was something to do when it seemed I couldn't do anything else. Later, one of the mothers told me that not all the mothers were revolutionaries and probably wouldn't use "Sandino" pillow cases. She suggested we give them to the comrades in jail instead, which we did.

During that period I began to work with women. We founded the Patriotic Organization of Nicaraguan Women, the predecessor to AMPRONAC. We organized peasant and working women. We worked to set up safehouses, raised money and agitated for better conditions in the prisons. Although I still couldn't pitch in full-time, I continued to become more active as my health improved.

I maintained contact with the Organization, mostly through the various comrades who visited me. But as I got better it became clear to me that the comrades weren't considering me for important tasks. They didn't think I was worth anything anymore. That hurt. I thought that the only way to prove I was ready and able to work was if I showed them I could still function as a normal person. My strategy was to find a lover and have another child. Then they'd realize I could do anything. But what kind of man would accept my life? Usually it's the woman who puts up with the man, but with me it was the other way around.

I met someone who wasn't politically active. He was against Somoza but didn't really understand what that meant. I really liked him—he was honest and sincere. And he was attracted to me. I worked hard to politicize him and I told him all about myself and my life. I needed to know his reaction so I'd have some indication whether he could handle the conditions my political work would create for us. I told him that there might be times when I'd have to go off and work with other men. He said he thought he could handle that kind of thing and I believed him. We began living together and shortly after that I became pregnant.

In March 1979 I was arrested for the last time. We had robbed a bank and unfortunately included some people who weren't committed to the Organization—they wanted the money for themselves. They observed minimal security measures which, in the end, resulted in the police being able to trace me. The FSLN got me a good lawyer and many people worked to get me out of jail. In 27 days I was on the streets again. By that time the final stage of the war was just beginning.

There is one experience I have to tell you about. Shortly after I was released from jail I was fighting near Chinandega. Things had gotten so bad we had to retreat toward Leon. We reached a farmhouse near the city and decided to send someone into Leon to make contact with the command there. I was chosen. Leon was in full-scale war by that time. A comrade lent me some clothes and I dressed as a peasant woman.

The comrade I met there didn't know who I was. How could the younger ones know all of us who had been struggling for such a long time? I explained my situation but just at that moment his squadron pulled out. He made the mistake of leaving without reporting my presence to the rest of the comrades. Suddenly I heard an order to transport prisoners. As it happened, I was sitting right there with the prisoners. No one asked who I was; I think they just assumed...

They blindfolded me. At first I didn't think a thing about it. We old-timers are used to observing security measures with no questions asked. It's second nature now. I thought they were working together well and taking full security precautions. Imagine the situation: I'm blindfolded and there's gunfire and bombing going on all around us. When we got near San Felipe I began to suspect that things weren't quite right. By then I realized I'd been mistaken for a prisoner. I was furious. We reached our destination and I demanded to be taken to the High Command.

When they finally removed our blindfolds I recognized one of the comrades. And when he realized who I was he was shocked. But that wasn't the moment to discuss the mistake. We had to attack the main problem. The leadership agreed to give me an armed squadron to go back and rescue the people we'd left behind. Finally I was functioning normally again. I was put in charge of an area between Leon and the San Antonio Sugar Mill.

I've always been interested in the problems of organizing peasants. Before the victory I worked to draw peasants into the revolutionary process. Many did participate, they worked hard to support us. During the war the FSLN knew it was crucial that we work with the peasants to ensure that crops and livestock would be saved so there would be food when the war was over.

Now I'm working for INRA.* I'm managing a commune near Poneloya. It is dedicated to the memory of the heroes of Pancasan. Setting up that commune has been hard work. We began with a small farm called El Pilar which the Nicaraguan Agricultural Institute gave us. And today, as a result of a very long and complicated struggle, the commune includes a larger ranch which originally belonged to a Somoza supporter.

Right after we arrived at El Pilar we started hearing all kinds of "lovely" rumours about the rancher next door. He had treated the peasants in this area terribly. We informed INRA and the Attorney General's office and they said they would investigate. They told us we should hold off on any action of our own. The ranch owner, however, had the peasants so angry that they decided to take the ranch by force. Their first plan was to destroy it, but we convinced them that that wasn't the answer. We couldn't stop them from carrying out the raid and in the long run it turned out to be a good decision. It gave us the opportunity to find papers linking the owner to the murderous State Security.

We photocopied all the material and passed on the originals to the Attorney General's office and INRA. A month later the documents had disappeared from both offices. Of course it makes sense that there would be some

* INRA was the National Institute of Agrarian Reform during the first few months of revolutionary power. Now Agrarian Reform is a government ministry.

confusion during the first few months after the war. There were still a good many people in the state apparatus who wanted to protect their class and family interests. But we still had our copies of the papers so we were able to keep fighting for our right to the ranch.

Even while the legal battle was going on we were occupying the ranch. We ploughed the earth and began to plant. We had the valuable help of a comrade who was a graduate agronomist. He gave us good advice from the beginning. We didn't think about just our own immediate needs but tried to plan in terms of the general needs of the national economy. We planted basic crops and exports too. Today we have 40 *manzanas** of corn, 60 of sesame seed, and 10 of pepper and melon combined. We also have 150 head of cattle.

The ranch owner continued to cause us problems. He had friends in professional and administrative positions. The first trial favoured him and he began to put pressure on us to get off "his" farm. But we had faith in the FSLN leadership and in the Revolution; we knew that as our new government consolidated itself it would become clear who had rights to what. The problem was that the process moved so slowly. Once again we took our documents to the Attorney General and INRA. Things went differently that time, although again INRA told us to leave, just until things could be legalized—then we could return. We told them we weren't willing to leave; we'd won the Revolution and weren't going to retreat.

The whole thing got very complicated and at times it seemed to turn into a personal battle between me and the rancher. He went to the Ministry of the Interior and began spreading lies about me. He went so far as to accuse me of shooting him in the lung. I'd never even seen the man in my life. The Ministry of the Interior passed the report on to the Sandinist People's Army, and the military police called for an investigation. That was fine with me. I told them that if the rancher had come to our commune I'd have shot him in the head not the lung, and from that moment on the

* A *manzana* is four-and-a-half square blocks.

bourgeoisie would have to think twice about harassing peasants. The investigation proved that the guy had not been shot, by me or anyone else. This decision was a victory for all of us. It meant we had a legal right to our commune, and on December 2 we held our official inauguration.

Nine
Mothers and Daughters

> ...we think back through our
> mothers if we are women.
> —VIRGINIA WOOLF

Mother and daughter: traditionally, a difficult relationship. All women are daughters and most eventually become mothers. The profound joy of giving birth is, however, almost always marred by the real problems of the society into which the child is born. Every child born to a working class or peasant family is another mouth to feed. Furthermore, becoming a mother is too often an ambition which parallels men's desire to be engineers or doctors, in short, to be successful. Men are encouraged to become *something* while women must be content to find good husbands, produce children and work hard to serve them both.

This is a dream held up by capitalist society and marketed as a consumer item. Reality is very different. In the dependent capitalism of Nicaragua a great number of women have been abandoned by their husbands and forced to take any kind of work to support their children. As a consequence, women are the majority of the wage-earning labour force in the lowest-paid sectors. But both in the elusive dream and in real life, women are still mothers and daughters. The relation between them is ambiguous and intense in any society. In Nicaragua this is all the more true as the relationship is being re-formed by the Revolution, and women's participation in it.

The mother-daughter relationship is extremely complex.

Mothers develop a special closeness with their daughters. Tradition almost always keeps the daughter close to home while the son is encouraged to relate to the outside world. If a mother feels satisfied with herself and her life, she often wants her daughter to be as upright, as ethical, as good a housewife, as attractive or self-sacrificing as she. If a mother feels unsuccessful she may demand that her daughter become what she could not. She tries to "live again" vicariously through this young image of herself. The daughter then, is under constant, sometimes silent pressure to conform to the dream which is transmitted through her mother's ambitions.

Mothers expect that their daughters, too, will be mothers. It is both myth and goal. The young girl must grow sufficiently passive and dependent to attract a proper suitor. She must learn to be a good wife and mother and to ready herself to pass on to her own children the moral, religious, social and sexual values which she learned from her mother. As Simone de Beauvoir put it, "My mother's whole education and upbringing had convinced her that for a woman the greatest thing was to become a mother of a family; she couldn't play this part unless I played the dutiful daughter..."*

In this way a perpetual chain is projected into the future. A woman bears another woman, who in turn will be called on to live and suffer and repeat—with the modifications of her time and space—the same life cycle. The relation between mother and daughter is more than just an umbilical cord which connects all parents with their offspring. It is another—special, terrible—cord through which the nature of the most exact likeness runs. Adrienne Rich tells us that, "Mothers and daughters have always exchanged with each other—beyond the verbally transmitted love of female survival—a knowledge that is subliminal, subversive, preverbal—the knowledge flowing between two similar bodies, one of which has spent nine months inside the other..."†

* *Memoirs of a Dutiful Daughter*, Penguin Books Ltd., Harmondsworth, Middlesex, England, 1963, p.106.
† *Of Woman Born*, Bantam Books, New York City, 1977, pp. 220-221.

Even in these years of women's growing consciousness it isn't always easy for a daughter to see her mother as a woman and human being. She is first and foremost *Mother*. In Nicaragua this tradition has been challenged as more and more daughters assume leadership roles outside the home *and* with their mothers. In countless cases mothers began participating in the struggle as a result of their children's attitudes and activities. Of course it is not unheard of for the mother to be the first to become politically active. And then there are cases in which mother and daughter became active independently of one another. The specifics are always different but each of the mothers and daughters I talked with described a dramatic shift away from the traditional mother-daughter relationship.

Because Nicaragua's young people have undeniably assumed the leading role in the struggle, it has more often than not been a daughter or son who gradually led a mother to realize her potential as an independent and political person. This dynamic is eloquently expressed in the chapter on "The Commanders," especially in the case of Commander Monica Baltodano and her mother Zulema.

Early in her life Zulema was concerned with the need for social justice, but she began to participate only when faced with the choice of supporting her daughter's commitment or abandoning her. What is most powerful in her testimony is her conscious, step by step struggle with her own fear. Zulema had moments in which fear was her primary emotion and she felt burdened by her daughter's activity. Then, when Monica was imprisoned, Zulema's fears that her sympathies might be found out were superseded by her concern for her daughter. "I didn't care if the whole world knew I was a revolutionary."

Today she speaks with pride not only of her own participation but of that of her nine children as well. "Toward the end, what happened was what was bound to happen. All my children left home, every last one. They all became involved in the struggle." These are not idle words. Zulema lost her sixteen-year-old daughter in a bombing,

Lea Guido is Minister of Social Welfare in the new National Reconstruction Government. Her mother, Dona Eva, sells meat in Managua's huge Eastern Market.

looked after another daughter whose hands were severed making contact bombs, and lived for months without knowing if Monica was alive or dead. "It helped being more politically aware. It helped later when I had to bear up under the hard blows I received. If I hadn't been clear politically I might have reacted the way many mothers did. Some are still resentful. It's their lack of political consciousness."

Zulema also gives us a glimpse of the mother-daughter/

mother-mother relationship when she describes her own mother's death. Her mother died while Monica was in prison. Zulema felt the pull of two obligations: that of remaining beside her elderly, dying mother and that of being present at such a crucial time for her daughter. "The morning my mother died she was listening to the radio and got wind of Monica's situation. She said, 'they didn't let the baby go...they didn't let her go...' But she couldn't really understand what was happening. She belonged to the world of the past."

In Lea Guido's office, there is a singularly beautiful photograph of a dark woman with deep-set eyes. She is standing beside a floral arrangement, and her long skirt is covered with flowers as well. "My mother's mother," Lea explained. "She sold meat in the Eastern Market too." Lea's own mother Eva sells meat in the same market. These references are reminders of the links between grand-mothers/mothers/daughters.

One woman I interviewed spoke about her first real contact with her mother outside the traditional maternal relationship. "I always got along with my mom, but the problems started when I began working politically. She noticed I was sneaking out and not telling her where I was going. She didn't understand what was going on, and I didn't feel I could talk to her about it. Things changed when she became involved herself. Then later, when we were both taken prisoner, the conflict between us dissolved. We could relate to each other as militants and comrades. Now we're good friends."

That's Rina Campos, the oldest daughter of Ruth Mercenaro. The relationship between Ruth and her two daughters illustrates a new and not uncommon situation among mothers and daughters in Nicaragua. Ruth is 38. She has been a member of the Sandinist National Liberation Front since 1975. She has four children: three daughters and a son. She's been separated from her husband for twelve years.

Ruth was a social worker in 1975. She worked with

peasants in Jinotepe, and it was their daily struggle for survival which opened her eyes to the living conditions most Nicaraguans faced. Looking for a way to become politically active, she tried to make contact with the FSLN. If she had been a student it would have been easy to join. But by today's standards she was an "older woman" and it took time to make the necessary contacts.

"I was always on the lookout for a chance to connect with the Front. But it was an underground organization and it seemed impossible to make contact. Finally though, I did get a chance. The Guard had killed a number of young people in our area, and everyone—except us social workers—spoke out against the murders. The leadership of the Social Workers Association was very conservative. They were not interested in denouncing injustice; they were hard and fast Somoza people. To circumvent them I started a petition on behalf of the university's School of Social Work and went to the campus to collect signatures. I wanted to convince others that everyone should raise a voice in protest. I took the petition to the university Student Centre and that's where the FSLN found me. It was the opportunity I'd been waiting for for a long time." Ruth joined the FSLN almost immediately.

It was easier for Ruth's oldest daughter to join. She was active in the student movement, and through that became involved in the 1972-73 truck drivers strike, the protest against the rise of the cost of milk, and the school sit-ins. She joined the FSLN in 1974, unaware of her mother's desire to be involved. She didn't even know when her mother became a member of the FSLN in 1975.

"I didn't know Rina was a member," Ruth confessed. "If I had I would have asked her to connect me with the Front. Nor did she find out until later that I had joined. We had to keep absolute discretion about those things, even within a family. It was rather strange. We both suspected something but neither of us said anything. I would notice that she hid things or tried to leave the house quickly at times, but I never said anything. And she suspected me too. The time came when we had a kind of silent pact; neither of us said, 'I think you are a member,' but we pretty well

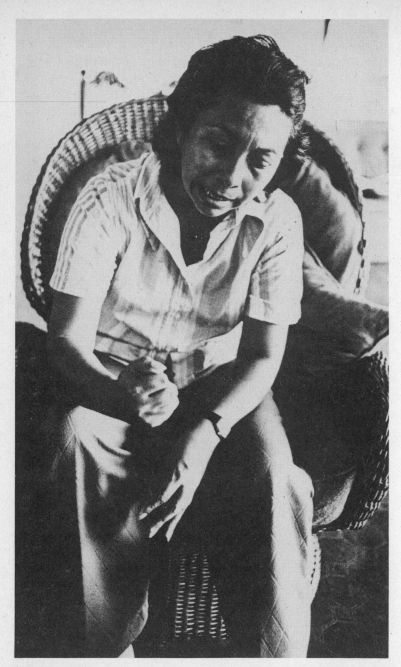

Ruth Mercenaro

knew. I was never really sure though until the repression came, and I saw my daughter in prison.''

Rina has her own version of that period. ''We were living in the house in La Centroamerica neighbourhood. Unknown to me, my mom joined the Organization in 1975. We kept our involvements from one another. When comrades came to the house, I would notice certain things. Mom's behaviour looked very familiar to me. And our discussions were more political than they had been. We analyzed the political situation from the perspective of militants. That was the way things were when we were both taken prisoner on February 4. . .''

The Guard arrested Ruth Mercenaro, her two daughters and her son. The son was fourteen and Ruth's other daughter—Maria Judith—was just ten. Their house in La Centroamerica had become a meeting place. On the day they were arrested, Commander Tomas Borge was meeting with other comrades at the Mercenaros'. Tomas succeeded in fleeing the house, but he was caught on his way out of the city. All but one of the other comrades managed to get away. Mildred Abaunza was killed.

It was in the dictatorship's State Security office that the two women—mother and daughter—realized the extent of each other's commitment. They were hooded, undressed, beaten and then chained to the walls of a filthy basement. They were kept naked for 26 days in an ice-cold room infested with rats and scorpions. Throughout, they were interrogated and threatened with the death of children and/or brothers and sisters.

''My mother didn't know they'd taken me too. She thought Maria Judith and I had escaped. But I knew the real story because I was the last to go. I could have denied any involvement since my mother had her name in her books—I could have said that the books and documents were hers. But of course I couldn't do that. I had to take responsibility for what was mine. I said I wasn't a member of the FSLN, just a sympathizer.

''They let my younger brother and sister go after a few days, but they kept my mother and me for almost a month. They forced us to do exercises, threatened us with rape, and subjected us to severe beatings. After the first few days, my mother and I were able to communicate with each other in hushed voices. We could lift our hoods just enough to make ourselves heard. That's when my mother first found out that they'd also taken my sister, and that Mildred had been killed. We couldn't touch each other but we could talk softly. We waited out the end of the tortures together.''

Both women were arrested again later. Ruth was in jail for fourteen months, Rina for nine. And in 1976-77 they spent much of the year being shifted back and forth between the State Security offices and the prison in Managua. When they got out of jail they continued their political work, and their mother-daughter relationship was strengthened by a common and deep bond of militancy.

Maria Judith, the youngest daughter, also has memories of their "family" experience. She is now fourteen and a member of the *July 19* Youth Movement. When she was taken prisoner with her mother and sister she was ten. She had never participated in any revolutionary activity. "It was such a shock," she recalls, "I couldn't even cry. I went blank. They asked me questions and beat me. I saw other prisoners being tortured.

"When I was in the patrol car my sister managed to tell me to say I didn't know anything. As soon as we got to the Security office they separated us and forced hoods over our heads. Later they stuck me in the cold room. I heard moans and realized I was there with two half-naked comrades who were covered with blood. But when I tried to get a look at them the guards hit me.

"After they removed me from that room they showed me photos of FSLN comrades and asked me if they had been in our house. I said no. They asked me if my mother and sister belonged to the Sandinist Front. I said no to everything. I saw my sister's glasses and imagined the worst. After a day my aunt showed up and they let me go. I went to my godmother's house and stayed there awhile. I returned to school and joined the MES (Secondary School Student Movement).

"My experience at the jail affected me for a long time. I was afraid when I saw comrades or when I saw guards. But

I did get involved through my school and also worked to improve my grades. My mother and sister were still in jail and I didn't want to let them down. I had been a poor student but I began to work harder at everything.''

Although it's been the influence of daughters on mothers that has been most common in Nicaragua, there are examples of the opposite. Mercedes Taleno and her daughter Lesbia Lopez lived in Open 3, a working class area on the outskirts of Managua. Mercedes is a thin, strong woman, every one of her 42 years marked on her worn face. When I interviewed her she was working in the Revolution's State Security Services and Supplies office, in charge of weapon control. But she missed her contact with people—especially women—and switched to the women's association.

Lesbia is now eighteen. Her elder daughter, Maura, is two years old. She was conceived when Lesbia was raped by a guard who tortured her in prison. I knew of Lesbia's rape and subsequent pregnancy, and of the discussion it provoked within the revolutionary movement. There were those who thought she should abort the child, as if paternity was the only issue. Another group, mostly women, took the opposite view: that the child would be the mother's and the baby a symbol of struggle and resistance, proof of women's capacity no matter what the risks or consequences.

Mercedes speaks without taking her eyes from yours. That gaze—sad, but profoundly steady—adds weight to her words. ''I arrived in Sandino City in late 1972 with my eight children. My husband never approved of my involvement in struggle. We separated two years ago for that reason. He always told me to stop taking part and think about my children. I told him it was precisely because I cared about my children that I had to participate. My husband resorted to friends and priests to persuade me to stay home but I was determined. Nothing could stop me. In 1973 I began working with Caritas.*

* Caritas is a Catholic charity organization with missions in many countries. Although many of its projects have negative as well as positive aspects, many women began confronting social problems through work with these groups.

Lesbia Lopez and her two-year-old daughter, Maura. Lesbia was raped by a guard in prison when she was sixteen. Maura's birth resulted from that experience.

"It was through my example that my children got involved, one by one. My oldest son Edgar was killed at the end of the war. I feel the satisfaction of my son giving his life to our country, though it's hard for me to say that. Someday it will be easier, I'm sure, but the wound is still too raw. I love our Revolution deeply. You can't imagine how deeply. I was willing to offer my life or freedom. Now I feel doubly committed; besides being ready to give my own life I've also sacrificed my son's.

"The enemy always looked at us as though we were

insignificant, but we aren't. The truth is that we are strong when we're together. I'm a simple woman, a woman with no schooling, but I knew I wanted to fight. And that's what I did. I always carried a gun with a bullet in the chamber, just in case. If the Guard caught me I wanted it to be dead, not alive. I planned to shoot at them and then kill myself. But the Guard never suspected me because of my age.''

In another culture Mercedes, at 42, would be in her prime. But in Nicaragua this woman was too old to arouse suspicion in the repressive forces. Thousands of ''old women'' like Mercedes played a decisive role in the struggle. ''Young people made this revolution, but you can't say that older people didn't take part. We older people were more afraid. We were afraid a son or a daughter might die or be taken prisoner. It's that selfish streak parents have. Many of us lacked political consciousness, but when we saw our children's commitment we had to commit ourselves. That was what happened in many families.''

Lesbia shifts the newborn in her arms and starts to talk. Her other daughter, Maura, follows her mother's every move with her enormous eyes. This eighteen-year-old woman describes how she was captured while putting up posters with another comrade. She relates a history—like so many—of torture, rape, the military court and prison.

Death has been a common denominator in her life: her brother's death, the deaths of all the comrades in her squadron and her own comrade's death. How could life be less than precious to her? The lives of her two daughters, each born under difficult circumstances, reaffirm her strength.

I asked Lesbia about the participation of women. It's clear their participation during the war was extraordinary, but I wanted to know what's happening now that peace has come. In other revolutionary processes men have been able to accept women's participation during the crisis; but when the war is won and old values come back into play men again demand women's servitude.

After hearing my concern Lesbia looked at me as though I were from another planet. ''If women are conscious, there won't be any problems like that. Their husbands might protest, there might be a slew of kids and tons of problems, but if women are conscious they will take part. They're participating now and they've got to keep going.''

There are many stories of mothers and daughters among the women I interviewed for this book. If it wasn't the daughter who gave form to the mother's aspirations, it was the mother who supported her daughter's involvement. And through that support developed a new perspective on life. It is impossible to exaggerate the transformation in the lives of tens of thousands of Nicaraguan women resulting from the revolutionary process in the past decade.

In the North, near Honduras, in the traditionally reactionary border town of Ocotal, they told us about Azucena del Rosario Antunez. She is the only woman who holds a position on the FSLN's departmental committee as well as on the local government Junta. When we got to the city hall, which sits on one side of the spotless central square, there was no mistaking her. From a sparsely furnished office emerged a 37-year-old woman: simple, direct, smiling. She was the only woman there, and she was waiting for us.

Azucena del Rosario has been a teacher all her life. ''I participated alone in the struggle, as an abandoned mother. I had a nine-year-old daughter and a son who wasn't yet three. My daughter began acting as a messenger when she was still practically a baby. She watched the doors of the house and warned us if anyone was coming. She always did it perfectly.

''I didn't have anyone to leave my kids with. My parents were in their seventies. If I'd been involved before my children were born I probably wouldn't have had any. Maybe it would have been me who died in the mountains and not my daughter. Her name was Veronica. She died at fifteen. I mean, we adults should have been able to give our children a free country, not the other way around.''

What Nicaraguan mothers bore throughout the years of

struggle surpasses the power of words. There are so many stories. There are so many parents who said goodbye to their children in the morning and never saw them alive again. Marina Solis is a widow who is familiar with hardship and poverty. Her involvement in her trade union gave her plenty of chances to witness the repressive tactics of Nicaragua's authorities. But nothing prepared her for the loss of her son.

"He was fourteen. I sent him to Matagalpa for his own protection. I knew they might kill him at any moment. And that's exactly what happened. They were just kids. They occupied Calvary Church in a peaceful sit-in. They didn't even have weapons. He said goodbye to me at six in the morning, saying 'Don't worry, mom, we're going to stage an act of civil disobedience, that's all.' By nine o'clock my son was already a corpse.

"I went out that day and was told Calvary Church was surrounded. I rushed straight over there. When the Guard spotted us, they moved in our direction, their guns raised...but I didn't back off. I kept walking and then I heard someone say, 'They killed every last one of them.' I went blank. They threw some of them from the bell tower and others down the steps. They even mutilated some of the bodies. It was a nightmare. When we got to the morgue to claim our children they made us pay 80 *cordobas* for each of them. They said, 'You have to pay us for the bullets these sons of bitches cost us.'"

As I talked with Marina I remembered something Commander Maria Tellez said, "How could values *not* change in families where loved ones were lost? What can't change? Anything, even the role of women—so deeply rooted—can change..."

But what about changing relationships among members of the bourgeoisie? Nicaraguan youth of all classes participated in the revolutionary struggle. Many of the young women I talked with had parents who showed differing degrees of understanding and identification. Martha Cranshaw is the daughter of a bourgeois family. Martha was captured, tortured and kept in solitary confinement for an unusually long period of time. When she finally saw her parents after her ordeal her father's reaction was to disown her.

Referring to that painful moment, Martha insisted, "I knew it was up to me to understand my parents, not them me. They couldn't understand. They couldn't understand why I had left my house and all its comforts to enter a world in which I didn't know where I would sleep at night or what I would eat. They couldn't comprehend my decision. It's our job to get them to understand, little by little, by our example."

Alexa Lugo is a young woman whose story illuminates the thread of decision and courage which runs so strongly through Nicaraguan women. Alexa Lugo was a guerrilla on the Northern Front. She began to collaborate when she was twelve and has been in the FSLN for a number of years.

I interviewed several young women with similar histories, women who had become involved at an extremely early age. They almost all gave sparse testimonies, as if it were difficult for these comrades to understand the importance of their personal experiences. Perhaps they have never really known anything else and simply don't consider their lives unique in any way.

I met Alexa at the Organization's *Juan de Dios Munoz* House in Managua. She had come south to consult on a series of problems related to her work in the *July 19* Sandinist Youth Movement. And as with so many others, I had to insist on the importance of hearing about her childhood, her family and how she entered the political struggle.

"I had a girl friend who was already involved and she told me about her experiences. My mother also talked to me about what was really going on in our country. At that age, you're not thinking about repression or whether there's a bourgeoisie and a proletariat. You don't think about things like that. But gradually, through these conversations and my contact with working class women in Matagalpa, I began to understand.

Alexa Lugo

"When I had a plate of food, something I liked, I would sit and think about the comrades in the Schick neighbourhood who had nothing to eat. And we wasted food. That's how my ideas began to develop, from simple things. Our family has always been very close: my mother, brothers and sisters. . . and we all joined the FSLN.

"Girls my age, shit, their greatest ambition was to go to a party at the social club or to celebrate their fifteenth birthday at church with a Te Deum and fifteen ladies-in-waiting. But that no longer meant anything to me. I didn't have what you'd call a normal childhood. For me it was school, work, demonstrations, and repression. Finally I went to the mountains and joined the guerrilla. It was always my dream to join the FSLN.

"A few years ago, in Matagalpa, it was very hard to organize the other girls at my school—a school for upper class girls. The system still had a grip on them. They thought only about educating themselves so they could get a diploma and earn more money to be able to waste it on cars and new clothes. Slowly but surely, however, the young people in Matagalpa have shown more solidarity. First the working class kids, then the others. Now we are all comrades, we're all united. And some of those same girls are now members of the Sandinist youth organization. That's what's important now. We've forgotten the rest. All the offences belong to the past, the pages of history that went with the dictatorship."

What conclusions do we reach from all this? Can we say that the old mother-daughter relationships no longer exist in Nicaragua? Of course not. The return to normality after a time of crisis always carries with it a certain return to old values. When those who had their customs wrenched from them have the chance to clutch them again they do so with the urgency of one seeking refuge in a known and loved place. I think that the key here is *consciousness*. Those who were removed from their familiar context by force and against their will tend to return to it. But those who consciously chose one path over another did so to affirm something that was in line with their changing values.

In this dramatic transformation of values and human relations we can clearly differentiate the vanguard from the masses. They have neither the same options nor the same consciousness when making their choices. They are in different though related situations. The militant knows what she did before and why; what she is doing now and why. Another woman may have been thrust into a similar situation because her fighting or class instinct told her she should, but she may not have internalized it as a positive turn in her life. Perhaps she sees it as a necessary and temporary sacrifice.

New experiences themselves begin to create new values. Rituals which once held great importance now have little meaning. Before, a woman might have said to herself, "I'll die if I don't get married in white..." or "you do what your dad says." But in the mountains, in the guerrilla camps, a couple were married walking between two rows of crossed rifles. Many took their solemn oaths, not before a priest, but before their own comrades in struggle. And more or less the same percentage of these marriages as of the traditional variety fell apart or lasted. In the long run the outcome didn't depend on the rituals.

In Nicaragua today there is an explosion of pregnancies. As in previous revolutions women feel the urge to reproduce and bring new life into a world which promises hope and justice. These pregnancies are not only occurring in the context of conventional marriages. Sometimes the husband isn't around—maybe he died fighting or the relationship ended—but the woman decided to have the child anyway. Or perhaps the relationship continues but the woman and man are separated because they are working on different fronts. As traditional couple relationships are being re-examined in the context of the revolutionary process women are demanding, and now attaining, new and equal status.

Not only couple relationships are acquiring new dimensions. Others are being questioned as well. Mother-daughter relationships show changes resulting from women's experience in the struggle. A daughter who made contact bombs, led a squadron, or was in the mountains for two years is no longer "mother's girl who doesn't know what she's doing and must be home by nine." And mothers too have changed. Women of 50 and older joined, showing themselves capable of organizing essential support services—that can't be overlooked. What about daughters and mothers who fought together? Can they ever see each other in the same light again?

I want to close this chapter with a letter written by Idania Fernandez. Her war name was Angela. She was 24 when she was killed by the National Guard in Leon on April 16, 1979. A month before her death she wrote these lines to her daughter Claudia. They remain a legacy from all revolutionary mothers to all children.

March 8, 1979
My dear daughter:
This is a very important time for people everywhere; today in Nicaragua, and later in other countries in Latin America and throughout the world. The Revolution demands all each of us has to give, and our own consciousness demands that as individuals we act in an exemplary way, to be as useful as possible to this process.

I hope that someday, not too far off, you may be able to live in a free society where you can grow and develop as human beings should, where people are brothers and sisters, not enemies. I'd like to be able to walk with you, holding hands, walk through the streets and see everyone smiling, the laughter of children, the parks and rivers. And we, ourselves, smile with joy as we see our people grow like a happy child and watch them become new human beings, conscious of their responsibility toward people everywhere.

You must learn the value of the paradise of peace and freedom you are going to be able to enjoy. I say this because the best of our brave people have given their precious blood and they've given it willingly, with great love for their people, for freedom and for peace, for the generations to come and for children like you. They've given their lives so children won't have to live under this repression, humiliation and misery so many men, women and children have suffered in our beautiful Nicaragua.

I'm telling you all this in case I'm not able to tell you personally or no one else tells you these things. A mother isn't just someone who gives birth and cares for her child; a mother feels the pain of all children, the pain of all peoples as if they had been born from her womb. My greatest desire is that one day you will become a true woman with a great love of humanity. And that you'll know how to defend justice, always defend it against whatever and whomever would trample it.

To become this kind of person, read and assimilate the works of the great leaders of our revolution and of the revolutions of other countries, take the best of each as example and put these into practice so that you will continue to grow always. I know you'll do this and that you can do it. And that gives me great peace.

I don't want to leave you words, promises or empty morals. I want to leave you an attitude to life, my own (although I know it isn't yet the best) and that of all my Sandinist brothers and sisters. I know you will learn how to use it.

Well, my plump one, if I have the privilege of being able to see you again—which is also a possibility—we'll have long talks about life and the Revolution. We'll work hard carrying out the tasks we're given. We'll play the guitar and sing and play together. And through all this, we'll come to know each other better and learn from one another.

Come, show me your pretty face
Lovely like flowers and freedom
And give me energy to struggle
Uniting your laughter and our reality
Daily I think of you
Imagining always how you are
Always love our people, and humanity

With all the love of your mother, Idania.
   Until our victory, forever.
   Free Homeland, or Death.

Ten

Profound Changes

Revolution is the only force capable of transforming the structure of society. After years of exploitation, people become part of a painful but extraordinary process through which they break the chains of dependence and begin to participate as "architects of their liberation."* The political change which took place in Nicaragua opened up the possibility of structural changes in every area of life. The changes in institutions, values and attitudes that are underway right now are themselves a continuation of the revolutionary process; they will likely prove as gruelling as the revolutionary struggle itself.

The breakdown of traditional values has been violent. In the midst of revolutionary struggle, time loses all meaning, forcing dramatic shifts in people's outlook and practice in a matter of days and weeks, not years. Old solutions are no longer valid; critical problems call for new answers. Things that once seemed important and urgent are forgotten as people mourn the loss of those closest to them: a lover, a son, a daughter. In building the new society, the survivors find new ways to live that develop new and collective values.

In each of the more than 80 interviews conducted for this book I was confronted with people's growing ability to

---

* From the FSLN anthem.

become active participants in change, on both personal and social levels. Almost every conversation revealed signs of transformation and growth as women developed new ways of relating to other women, to lifelong comrades, to their children and to themselves. This chapter contains interviews with four women whose experiences, although very different from one another, reflect these changes in particularly dramatic ways.

Melania Davila *spoke with us in the small living room of her wooden shack in a poor section of Leon. It was mid-morning, and two young children—studying for their afternoon classes—shared the only bench, leaning their notebooks against a bed obviously used by the entire family. A small girl clutched at her mother's skirt as we talked. Two photos stood out among the old calendars, patriotic and religious symbols on the walls. Both were reminders of her second son, who was seventeen when he was killed during the last month of the war. The first showed a young determined face, his eyes those of his mother. The other was a photo of Melania and comrades surrounding the son's coffin, covered with the red and black flag of the FSLN.*

Melania was a prostitute at eighteen. As in most cases, her decision was not a voluntary one. She had few options. She travelled that difficult and painful road with bitterness and never resigned herself to her situation. One day, seven years ago, she came into contact with the Sandinist National Liberation Front and new possibilities opened for her.

MELANIA: My real name is Melania Davila, but I used "Maribel" on the street. We'd change our names not realizing that people would recognize us anyway. My family comes from San Miguelito de Contales, in Rio San Juan. My parents separated when I was six months old and I was left with my mother. But she was very poor and in the end was forced to send me to my aunts. They treated me like dirt and continually humiliated me. I grew up feeling like I was nobody. To get away from them I went off with a man who worked in the capital.

I married that man just after I turned thirteen. I had two children with him, Silvia and Francisco. I left my husband when he joined the National Guard. I never wanted to have anything to do with anyone in the military. When I left him Silvia came with me and he took Francisco. I never saw my son again; he'd be 23 now. After that I started living with another man. He was no better. He beat me terribly. I stayed with him three long bitter years. We had two children—Delimo, who was killed last year, and Maria de los Angeles. But finally I couldn't stand it any longer and had to leave.

That's when I began working the streets to support myself and my children. One of my neighbours offered me a job as a waitress and I took it to earn some extra money. It turned out that it wasn't a waitress they wanted. That's how I got into that kind of work. After I left home it was the only way I could support us. I went to Granada and worked out of a house run by a very wicked woman they called "La China." She beat me all the time and rigged things so that none of us got paid. There were about fifteen of us in the house. They'd dress us in second-hand clothes and if we complained they'd let us have it. They tried to make us completely submissive. They'd lock us in when we weren't working so we couldn't get away. Finally I was able to escape. I went to Managua and started working in the Campo Bruce district. At least I got paid there and so was able to send my oldest daughter to live with my mother. Neither of them had the slightest idea where my money came from.

The FSLN changed my life. That was seven years ago, here in Leon. I met comrades Azida and Abel, who is dead now, and through them I started working with the Organization. We collected and sent foodstuffs and medicines to the mountains. We used to store all sorts of clandestine material in my house, despite the fact we lived next door to a woman whose husband was in the National Guard. She used to threaten to denounce us as Sandinistas but I told her, "Go ahead and do it. You'll be sorry! You'll soon learn just what the FSLN is made of.''

It was terrible when my son was arrested. The Guard demanded I pay 1,200 *cordobas* for his release. When I

Malania Davila

went to get him the first time, they asked if I knew my son had taken part in the fighting that September. I had to act surprised. They were killing a lot of kids and I was afraid for his life. I said, "No, my son's not a Sandinista. Please let him go. I'm just a poor washerwoman who earns an honest living." They said they'd let him go but first I'd have to pay 2,000 *cordobas*. I couldn't afford that much and pleaded with them to take less. They finally agreed to 1,200 *cordobas*. I just paid back the last 80 *cordobas* last month, and my son's been dead for seven months now.

After his release my son got involved again almost immediately. On the morning he left he told me not to worry. "Don't cry if I don't come back," he said. "Consider yourself lucky to have given a son to the FSLN and our country. If I don't live to enjoy the new life it will be there for my younger brothers and sisters and all the other children that do survive." He was only seventeen years old. He died fighting at La Leona, the fortress outside Leon. It was Sunday July 8 at 1:30 in the afternoon. Leon was liberated and my boy died.

I look older than 39 because I've worked hard all my life and have suffered a lot. I'm tired of washing and ironing—I want to live a different life. Despite my age I want something new. Everything's different now that we've won. We walk freely in the streets without fear of being killed. There are new possibilities for everyone. I had to learn to read and write all on my own but now I can go to school. Now even women will be able to study.

I belong to the FSLN and the women's association. We'll have to work hard for a long, long time. But you, the younger generation, will have a different life. I think often of what my son said when he left. I tell other mothers not to cry and to think about the schools and hospitals we're going to have. It's through these kinds of things that our fallen sons and daughters will remain alive.

The next woman I spoke with was Marisol Castillo. *On December 27, 1974, while her parents were giving a party for the U.S. ambassador, an FSLN commando broke into her home. Marisol was eighteen at the time. Her father lost his life in that action, yet Marisol was able to accept that the commando had no other choice when her father resisted. Much has happened since that night. For Marisol, that night of hostages and Sandinistas was followed by experiences of repression, struggle, death and victory.*

The political polarization which forced Nicaraguans to take sides in the struggle was particularly painful for the Castillos. Marisol's mother and brother fled to the United States. The two daughters stayed to fight. Marisol began to work with the FSLN through the student movement and later joined the Front. She married Edgard Lang, another Sandinista of bourgeois origin, who was killed in Leon in April 1979. Marisol survived—with a small child to raise and a country to rebuild. She currently works in the Sandinist army. I interviewed Marisol on the fifth anniversary of the FSLN action at her family's house.

MARISOL: I had an easy, carefree childhood, similar to most children in bourgeois families. We lived in Managua until my father started working with the World Bank, when we moved to Washington for five years. Then we returned to Nicaragua. I had always lived a life of luxury but if you live in a country like ours you can't help but feel the contradictions of your wealth. The poverty is incredible, the slums. . . you live in a world of riches fully aware of how the "other half" lives.

The incident at our house was my first formal contact with the FSLN. By that time I was active in the Christian movement and my boyfriend Edgard Lang was an FSLN supporter, but I'd never had any direct contact with the FSLN and didn't really understand what it was all about. It was only by chance that I was home when the FSLN commando arrived at our house. I'd planned to be out for the evening. It was quite an experience. All of a sudden we heard shots and then there was total chaos. Some people thought the noise was firecrackers but I knew right away it was shots. I was scared to death. Everyone was running

around. I hid in the bathroom. Somoza's son Leonel and
Jose Somoza were also in there with me. They tried to
convince me not to go out but I had to see what was going
on. When I came out, I was lined up against the wall with
the others. I was so scared I could barely stand.

Hugo Torres was standing guard over us. I didn't know
Hugo then but later he told me that he was really nervous
too. He saw that I was trembling. German Pomares was in
charge of the military part of the action. I was particularly
scared of him. He seemed so severe. His face and expression
made it clear that he was a man who'd never give in. But
later, when I got to know him, I discovered that he was the
kindest, most gentle man I'd ever known. At the time I only
recognized one member of the commando, Javier Carrion.
He's been a friend of mine since I was ten. But I'm getting
ahead of myself. At the time, all I felt was fear. But after
being held prisoner for awhile you lose your fear. Whatever
happens, happens. Everything is out of your control. It
wasn't until the next day, when we read the Front's
communique, that we found out exactly what was going on.
I was overwhelmed by the contradictory emotions.

You asked about my father's death. My father was a very
violent man. He always said if someone attacked him he'd
defend himself with force. When I was in the bathroom I
heard that someone had been killed and I immediately
suspected it might be my father. We weren't told what
happened but later, when I didn't see my father anywhere, I
was sure that something had happened to him. My mother
and sister Patricia were nowhere to be seen and I was
worried that they might also be dead. It turned out they
were hiding on the patio. They didn't come out till six the
next morning.

I never blamed the FSLN for killing my father. Naturally
when someone you love dies you feel it deeply, but I knew
he was a violent man and that the same thing could have
happened to him in any political situation. It was more
difficult for my sister Patricia, but later she was able to
understand too. My brother and mother never accepted it;
now they live in Washington. I don't think they'll ever
understand. My separation from them has been very

difficult but there was no choice. There are times in your life when your political ideas cut you off from certain things. My life and goal became the triumph of the Revolution and my family became less important. The Revolution had to come before my family.

After the December 27 action I began to get closer to the FSLN and by 1976 I was an active collaborator. Edgard went to fight in the mountains and I went to Washington to finish my degree. While I was in the U.S. we formed a solidarity committee to do support work. By 1978 I was back in Nicaragua working as a messenger and chauffeur. I was a full-fledged member by then and worked organizing different cells. I was totally immersed and assumed more and more responsibility as time went on. There was so much work to be done, but it was very hard because the repression was so fierce.

Edgard was arrested in November 1977 and released with the other political prisoners when the FSLN commando took over the Palace in August 1978. After that we both ended up in Panama where we stayed till early 1979. Edgard went back to Nicaragua in February and I followed in March. He worked on the Western Front and I stayed here in Managua. By that time I was pregnant and getting bigger every day. Curiously enough, I was able to enter the country legally. I spent a week in "cold storage," as we call it, to make sure I wasn't being watched. Once I was sure no one was following me I went back to work.

Edgard was killed in Leon on April 16, 1979 when I was four months pregnant. We brought his body back to Managua for the funeral. We marched through the streets with his coffin shouting slogans. The Guard was everywhere but nothing happened.

July 19, 1979 was an unforgettable day. We all went down to the square to watch the columns enter Managua. The columns from the different fronts arrived separately and it was incredibly moving to see how many comrades were still alive. It seemed almost unreal. After fighting so hard we had really won. There were times when everything seemed so difficult and victory seemed so far away. We all knew we'd win one day, but. . .

I joined the army a few days after the triumph. I was seven months pregnant. Now I'm in charge of the cadre-training section. My daughter Martina is three months old. Edgard's middle name was Martin, and since Edgarda sounds awful, I called her Martina. She lives with me although I hardly ever see her. The Revolution must come before our children and families. We've got a whole country to rebuild.

On Nicaragua's remote Atlantic coast, in the city of Puerto Cabezas near the Siuna mines, a little girl was born and grew up to become known through the region as "Siuna nun." Dorothea Wilson comes from a part of Nicaragua that has always been isolated and where life is especially difficult. The people speak more English or Miskito than Spanish. The war didn't touch this part of Nicaragua.

Dorothea is the only woman in the local government of Puerto Cabezas. We went to speak with her and ended up following her in her daily tasks, which that day included dealing with the problems of food distribution, attending a planning meeting for the literacy crusade and taking care of a number of different issues at city hall. We finally managed an interview at 11:30 p.m.

DOROTHEA: I was born in the northern part of Zelaya in Puerto Cabezas, the region's second largest city. There were seven children in our family. My father worked for over 35 years in the mines, and my mother was a maid.

Like many Nicaraguan girls, I studied in a Catholic school. I was always around the nuns and one day I just decided to join the Carmelites of the Divine Heart of Jesus. I was there for two years, working in missions alongside the poor. It was hard at first. I'm a very active person and always felt a bit frustrated by the contemplative life. Eventually though, I got used to it. Later I decided to leave the Order and continue my work with peasants outside the convent. I left in 1974 when I was 24.

Five of us left together to set up a religious communal life dedicated to working with the people. We worked mainly in the mountains with peasant women, trying to help them better their lot. It turned out we were right in the heart of the guerrilla zone. I continued the religious life for two more

Dorothea

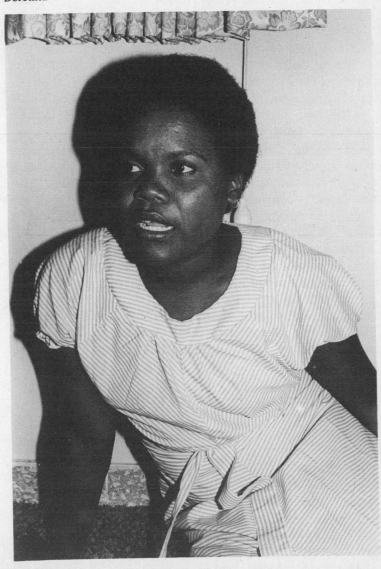

years. But during that time I began to work more and more closely with the guerrillas. We didn't wear habits or veils, but we were called missionaries, which meant we could move quite freely around the area.

My religious work more and more became a cover for political work. The National Guard was all over the area and that was the only way we could do political work. Even so they caught on to us. That forced us to choose between continuing the so-called religious life and joining the guerrilla. I decided to stay in the mountains with the guerrilla. From the moment I made that decision I abandoned my religious life completely. For the time being I'm still a believer although I've gone through many changes and am still changing.

Three of the five of us who left the convent opted to devote ourselves full-time to the struggle. Today, one is the FSLN representative in the local government in Siuna. The other recently returned to the Order and is now training novices. I represent the FSLN in the government Junta here in Puerto Cabezas.

I had already been a member of the Front for some time when I joined the guerrilla. I remember once we took Henry Ruiz—Commander Modesto—into the city for a meeting of the FSLN leadership. We travelled with him for a week, passing him off as a seminary student. I was involved in some military actions but mostly I worked as a messenger transporting supplies from abroad to the mountains. I made four trips to Costa Rica and Panama. We were very ingenious in getting stuff into the country. We packed radios, microphones and transmitters in paint cans or stuffed them into the busts of plastic figurines. We even used commercial airlines to transport ammunition wrapped as Christmas presents.

The religious community gave us a lot of support. Mail from abroad was transported directly to the mountains solely by priests and nuns. In Chiriqui and even Panama I met nuns and priests who collaborated in every way possible. They carried out very dangerous tasks, often not knowing whether they'd come back alive.

Now that we've won there is much work to be done in this

area Somoza used to call his fortress. (He even threatened to launch a counter-revolutionary attack from here.) Our work has to be intense and very thorough. We must first give people land and seed, then we can talk. Then we can "Sandinize" them. Remember, there was no struggle here, not one shot was fired in the whole region. When we entered the city, the National Guard had already fled. The people had weapons and they turned in their arms when we reached the city.

For the past 150 years the population here has been marginalized, discriminated against and completely separated from the rest of the country. Comrades in other areas know nothing about conditions here. The National Reconstruction government considers this a top priority zone. There's a special development plan for the area aimed at increasing production; we have all the resources—land, cattle, everything. This is virgin land and will be a great source of employment. There's going to be a tremendous effort made here...

Carmen Azucena Rodriguez Prado is a 21-year-old woman who works in the office of Commander Monica Baltodano. Simple, strong, with an open expression and tender eyes. Carmen was a policewoman during the Somoza regime. She entered the "peace-keeping" force quite young, with the idea of working with delinquents. Her interest was social work, but she soon realized that Somoza's police force dealt in repression and brutality, not people's welfare. By then it was too late.

Carmen met Monica in jail. Monica was the prisoner, Carmen the guard. The contact between the two was a consciousness-raising experience for Carmen. Ultimately it led her to join the FSLN. Of the four women in this last chapter, Carmen's transformation is perhaps the most dramatic. Not only did she go from being a policewoman to a revolutionary militant, but she undertook the dangerous task of operating for two years on the inside of one of the most brutally repressive forces in Latin America.

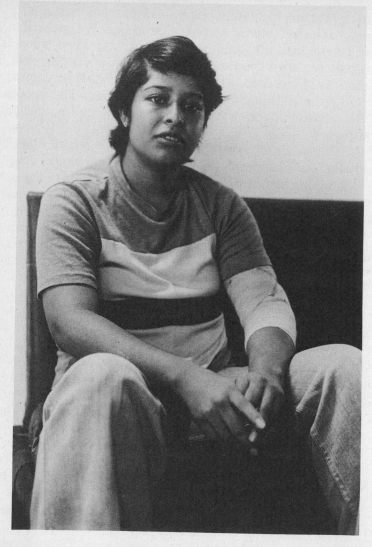

Carmen

CARMEN: My family was what you might call middle class. My father was a professor and school principal; my mother was a housewife. There were eleven kids and I was the next to last. I didn't really choose to enter the police force. I was in my third year of high school and wanted to keep studying. But my father wasn't living with us anymore and I had to start helping support the family. Every job I applied for, except the National Guard, required at least a high school degree. The Guard said junior high was enough and they would allow me to keep studying and earn a salary at the same time. They said they'd help us get ahead. Even though it wasn't what I wanted I had to have some kind of job so I signed up. That was 1975.

We learned about things like traffic control, criminal investigation and how to deal with the public. I graduated from the course in 1976 and began to work immediately. We did a stretch in each of the different sections as part of our training. At that time they were looking for people with teaching experience to work in the juvenile court which had just opened. I was one of five women they selected.

I was filled with illusions about those kids. They're the ones who roam around the markets, sniffing glue and all that. We took care of them, took them to the hospital when they needed it, gave them classes, etc. I really thought we could save them. I was straight out of the classroom and didn't know what being a cop was really about. I thought we were going to help and protect people.

After the juvenile bureau I worked at the bureau of investigations. That was where they started ordering me to mistreat people. I couldn't do it. I just couldn't raise my hand against anyone. After people were arrested, the women prisoners were brought to us. We were supposed to make them talk. They said beating was the only way.

I was always getting into trouble for not treating the prisoners the way they wanted me to. Once, Colonel Zamora left me alone with a female prisoner to "get the truth out of her." She was a maid who was accused of stealing some money. "I want to hear you," he said, "and I want to hear her scream." He gave me a hose to hit her with. When he left I sat down next to her and said, "Look what they've given me. I can't do it. It's better if you tell me..." But the woman started crying and said it wasn't true, she hadn't stolen the money. Zamora screamed that I was no good. He made me stay an extra week in investigations "to learn how to be a good policewoman."

He made me watch what they did to those poor women. I couldn't stand it and many times I ran out crying.

They were holding Monica in Matagalpa. Her guards were changed every two weeks. My turn came October 1. There were two of us. We'd sleep right in the jail, taking turns being on duty. Since I didn't know anyone in Matagalpa I stayed in the jail on my days off. That's when Monica began to talk to me. She asked me a lot of questions: why was I in the National Guard? did I like it? was I aware of the atrocities being committed? I told her why I joined and that I hadn't realized what it would be like until I started working. She said she was in prison because she was fighting to defeat Somoza and end the injustice of his regime. I began to admire her tremendously. The things she'd been through sounded horrible. She told me what they'd done to her when she was arrested. I admired her for her courage. She was willing to sacrifice her life so that some day we'd all be free.

I'm a person that feels for other people. I always argued with the other guards when they beat prisoners. When I worked in the juvenile section they used to call me "the mama" because I was the only one who defended the kids. Monica made me see the limitations of what I was doing. I could defend a few kids on the inside but what about the rest. She told me stories—horrible stories—about what the National Guard did in the mountains. I was really shocked. Slowly I became aware that I had to do something else. I began to think seriously about joining the FSLN.

Once I made the decision to join I had to move with discretion. Working for the Revolution within the Guard was very dangerous. If they ever found me out they would have killed me on the spot. At first I worked as a messenger, later I'd steal insignias, uniforms, arms and ammunition. I always had to be on guard. I even had to watch myself on the street. I could have easily been a target for an FSLN comrade. I couldn't say to anyone, "Look, I'm really on your side."

It was horrible in my family. My father backed Somoza, and one of my brothers was an officer in the Guard. Near the end they realized I was in the FSLN. My mother found some pamphlets I'd hidden in my room. She didn't say anything to me but she told my oldest brother and they decided to tell my brother who was the lieutenant. It turned out he already knew. He came home one day and said they'd caught on to me in Security. He claimed they hadn't arrested me because they wanted to find out who my contacts were. I told him I had known the risks when I decided to join the Front and he could be sure I wouldn't tell anyone anything. It was an ugly scene but I made it clear that I made my own decisions and wouldn't tailor my life or thinking to suit his career. He tried to pressure me but at least he didn't turn me in.

By 1978 we were preparing for the insurrection and work inside the Guard was getting too dangerous. My contact told me to find a way to get myself discharged. On May 15, 1978 I left the police and joined the insurrection. I was assigned to a place called La Pedrera, near Chinandega, where I worked mainly as a nurse.

Just before I left the police something happened that I'll never forget. A few of us were sent as "plainclothes" informers to a student demonstration. We were to find out who was armed, who the big shots were, who did most of the shouting, etc. We were to get all the information we could. I stayed toward the back of the march. A woman near me was carrying a flag and for some reason she dropped it. Someone grabbed me and said, "Here, take the flag." He thought I was a student. I was the last one in the row. Behind us were the guards. They were from other stations and didn't know me.

We began to march. "Shout, comrade," they yelled at me. The policewoman beside me whispered, "Prado, drop the flag." She knew, as I did, that the students were going to be arrested when they got to the university. The guards were there waiting for them and the students would be trapped between them and the guards following behind. That was when those of us undercover tried to get out. But as I tried to get away the guards started lobbing tear gas. The policewoman grabbed me but so did one of the students. "No comrade," the student said, "if we stay together they can't hurt us." It was horrible. Everyone was running to escape the tear gas, the shots, the arrests... The police were out to get me because they had seen me with the flag. Just when a guard was about to strike me the student grabbed me, and she got hit instead of me. I was trying to find my way out and this young woman was taking the beating meant for me. Through all this the woman kept clutchng onto me. The result was that we both got beaten. Finally the students were all rounded up and brought to the station. By that time the police had sorted out who I was.

It was awful when we got to the station. The policewomen had to register the women students and by chance I got the woman who had tried to defend me. She didn't say a word. All the sweetness in her face vanished when she saw who I was. She just kept glaring at me, not saying anything. Such hate in her eyes. Just imagine, she had taken a beating for me only to discover I was a cop. I've never seen her again but sometimes I walk around hoping I'll bump into her so I can let her know, now that we can speak freely, that we were on the same side.